MODERN AT MID-CENTURY:

The Early Fifties Houses of Ingraham and Ingraham

Elaine Freed

Foreword by Wim de Wit

The Hulbert Center for Southwestern Studies
Colorado College, Colorado Springs

Designer: Pamela A. Cosel

Freed, Elaine 1934—
Modern at Mid-Century: The Early Fifties Houses of Ingraham and Ingraham / Elaine Freed;
new photography by Ron Pollard

Includes bibliographical references and index.
ISBN 0-935052-40-2

Published in 2003 by The Hulbert Center Press, Colorado College, Colorado Springs, Colorado
All rights reserved. No part of the contents of this book may be reproduced without the
written permission of the publisher.

Colorado College—The Hulbert Center Press
Hulbert Center for Southwestern Studies
14 E. Cache la Poudre St.
Colorado Springs, Colorado 80903
www.coloradocollege.edu/dept/SW/

Printed in USA
Gowdy Printcraft
A division of American Graphics, Inc.

For my sons,

Casey Freed and David Freed

CONTENTS

Starting an architectural practice is not easy. Young, ambitious architects eager to establish themselves as independent designers soon discover that the creation of architecture is not only an artistic endeavor, as they might always have liked to believe, but it is also a business. One has to compete for jobs, which is no simple matter for someone who has not yet had an opportunity to make a name for him- or herself. Many first jobs are therefore kitchen renovations or extensions to houses. Lucky are those architects who have parents with the financial means to build a new residence, who are willing to take a risk, and who are supportive enough to help their child get his or her career off the ground by commissioning the building of a new house: numerous architects had their first breakthrough with the design and construction of a new house for their parents. The best-known example is probably Robert Venturi with his "Mother's House," but there are many others ranging from Frank Lloyd Wright (whose first job was not a house for his mother, but a school for his aunts) to Richard Meier and Charles Gwathmey.

Making a name for oneself during the 1950s must have been especially difficult. The entire architectural scene, both in the United States and in Europe, was controlled by the generation of architects who had come of age before the Second World War. In the United States there were two or three big names: Frank Lloyd Wright, Ludwig Mies van der Rohe, and, somewhat less established, Walter Gropius. Wright had an enormous influence, not only because he kept reinventing his architectural vocabulary, but also because, when he was already in his late eighties, he produced a number of buildings that were as high in quality as some of his well-known buildings designed in the 1920s and 1930s. The Guggenheim Museum in New York (1956), for example, can easily compete with the Administration building for the Johnson Wax Company in Racine, Wisconsin (1936), or with Fallingwater, the residence for Edgar Kaufmann, Sr., in Bear Run, Pennsylvania (1935). And Mies, having come to the United States in 1938 at the age of 52, designed a number of buildings, including Crown Hall at the Illinois Institute of Technology (IIT) in Chicago (1950–56) and the Seagram Building in New York (1954–58), which are counted among the key monuments of twentieth-century architecture.

Every architect tried to emulate these architects' work; in fact, certain critics tried to describe the American architectural world of the 1950s as a battle between two camps: the Wrightian organic architects versus the functionalist followers of Mies. While the architectural debate was obviously more complex than a dualistic division between two opposing philosophies, this critical characterization shows how encompassing was the influence of these two architects at the time. Given these circumstances, it should not come as a surprise that young architects had trouble finding their own identities. Add to this the notion that "marketing" was considered to be a dirty word in the mid-twentieth century. In fact, although both Wright and Mies were very good at "selling" their architecture, both preferred to present their work as an artistic creation only; business supposedly had nothing to do with it. Their students struggled with this lack of education in the practicalities of architecture for the rest of their professional lives.

Elizabeth Wright Ingraham and Gordon Ingraham were very much part of this culture: Elizabeth, the granddaughter of Frank Lloyd Wright, had studied with Mies at the School of Architecture at IIT. Gordon, her husband, had worked with Wright at Taliesin and knew the Wrightian vocabulary and philosophy intimately. One might have thought that young architects with such pedigrees would have "made it" relatively easily in the competitive world of architecture. But this notion may be more characteristic of the twenty-first century, when the star status of the architect has a much more substantial impact, providing a competitive edge to the work of his or her students. The pages that follow illustrate the fact that during the 1950s one could not necessarily count on having an advantage because of family relations. The Ingrahams had to struggle as hard as everybody else.

Little of historical nature has been written on the topic of establishing an architectural practice. It is therefore particularly satisfying that Elaine Freed, in the process of presenting the work of the Ingrahams, focuses on the couple's early work and their struggle to build up a clientele. She not only tells us about the houses that Gordon and Elizabeth Ingraham built in the late forties and early fifties, but also about the context in which they worked and why the social and cultural circumstances in Colorado made it so hard for them to keep the jobs coming to their young practice.

Freed's book is a tribute to the work of two remarkable architects; in addition, it provides an intelligent insight into the architectural climate of the mid-twentieth century. It tells us that the history of architecture of that period includes much more than the work of a few well-known designers, and that, in spite of what contemporary critics seem to think, the architectural scene was as rich and complex as that of any other time.

Wim de Wit, Head
Special Collections & Visual Resources
Curator of Architectural Drawings
The Getty Research Institute
Los Angeles

When I began examining the work of Ingraham and Ingraham, I was struck with the quality and appeal of their very early designs: those houses done for young clients of modest means. These early homes were so carefully articulated, so carefully situated, each one like a flower coming into bloom, that I marveled—not only over their singularity, but at their compatibility with each other. The Ingrahams's eldest daughter, Catherine, captured the character of her parents' houses when she described them as being like a family: "Their work was all of a piece—each one different but all related."[1]

I chose to concentrate on four Ingraham houses in Colorado Springs, Colorado, all designed and built within a four-year span from 1949 through 1952. Two are on a geological formation northwest of downtown called the Mesa, a table of land parallel to the foothills of Pikes Peak to the west and to Monument Valley Park to the east. Ten additional Ingraham houses were built in this same neighborhood during the 1950s, creating a minidevelopment, Mesa Terrace. The other two houses that I selected were about a mile away, situated on either side of the Colorado College campus, north of downtown Colorado Springs. All four are tucked into a hillside, sporting a hallmark flat roof and maintaining a very low profile. Hidden now by mature landscaping and self-seeding Siberian elms, the Mesa houses are hard to see from the street. All four homes are privately owned.

I first met the Ingrahams in 1960. Though never close friends, we shared interests and activities: politics, an educational program for international students, a cooperative nursery school. I saw them at parties and meetings—tall, talkative, vigorous, ready to laugh. They wanted to make the world a better place, and worked at it. Everyone knew that Elizabeth was related to Frank Lloyd Wright, but I seldom heard her talk about him except for occasional references to "grandfather." Her confidence, often read as arrogance, irritated some people.

During those years, I visited many Ingraham houses. I might have owned one myself, but even their comparatively modest cost was beyond my budget. During my undergraduate years at the University of Minnesota in Minneapolis, my fiancé and I often drove past Frank Lloyd Wright's Willey house near the university. I loved it from the start and when we moved to Colorado Springs in 1956, I transferred my modernist attachments to the Ingrahams's work.

Many years later, thanks in part to Elizabeth Ingraham's connections, I became executive director of the Frank Lloyd Wright Home and Studio Foundation in Oak Park, Illinois, and shortly after a vice president at the Frank Lloyd Wright Foundation based in Spring Green, Wisconsin, and Scottsdale, Arizona. These associations kept the Wrightian legacy foremost in my mind and kept me in occasional contact with Elizabeth. When I returned to Colorado Springs in 1990, I began thinking of writing a survey of the Ingrahams's work but did not begin in earnest until a decade later.

Gordon Ingraham died in the summer of 1999. I have recollections of him from earlier days but never formally interviewed him. Fortunately, he left an unpublished memoir that his family allowed me to read. These personal papers provided a wealth of material—facts about his life and work, but recollections as well about people, ideas, and values. Together with interviews with the Ingraham children—Michael, Catherine, Christine, and Anna—I was able to stitch together a sense of their family life, which was closely wedded to Gordon's and Elizabeth's professional work. In addition to these recent conversations, I relied on my memories of the children, all of whom I knew as they were growing up. In addition to the children, I was able to visit with Jacqueline Wright, who was married to Elizabeth's brother, John.

I interviewed Elizabeth several times. She graciously and generously opened the Ingraham and Ingraham firm's archives to me, and I was able to examine drawings, photographs, and correspondence. As a still-practicing architect who has moved on to design approaches different from Wright's and a departure from the earlier Ingraham and Ingraham work, she at first resisted my interest in the 1950s houses. She considered them to be derivative and backward looking. The Ingraham partnership produced eighty-five designed buildings, projects, and plans. Having thrown out the baby with the bathwater, perhaps she is reconsidering the early work and appreciates now, as so many of us do, the special quality of her professional achievements with Gordon.

My roster of Ingraham homeowner interviewees comprised E. R. and Judith Peterson [Wood-Peterson house], Martha Tilley [Tilley house], Robert and Mildred Beadles [Beadles house], Kent Borges and Stephanie DiCenzo [first Vradenburg house], Ardith Kensinger [Howbert house], Irving Howbert [Howbert house], Martha and Howard Whitlock [Whitlock house, Pueblo, Colorado], and Dawn and Brad Wilde [Wilde house, called "Solaz"].

I visited with Robert and Persis Smith, longtime residents of Colorado Springs, to get a sense of how the city has changed over fifty years. For information on the changing art world in the city, I interviewed John Hazlehurst, a writer and art collector, and Johanne Coiner, granddaughter of the artist Boardman Robinson. By telephone I spoke with artists Ellen O'Brien and Eric Bransby, as well as writer and teacher Hunter Frost, who wrote about Boardman Robinson. Finally, I met with Michael Collins, Morey Bean, and James Wallace, Colorado Springs architects, and by telephone I interviewed Dewey Dearing, another local architect.

In an afterword, I have included descriptions and photographs of Elizabeth's more recent architectural work. As well, there is an example of Gordon's colored-pencil drawings, which were a focus during his later years.

Even for a modest book, one relies on the help of a great many people. I was privileged to work with Ron Pollard, a Denver architectural photographer, on the four houses featured in the book. Marshall Kean provided organizational assistance from beginning to end. Lauren Arnest read and edited early drafts; Amy Brooks checked and proofread later versions. Lou Wynne guided me through the Ingraham and Ingraham Archives. Don Etter, author of several books on Denver architecture, offered guidance at the beginning, as did James Hartmann, former director of the Colorado Historical Society. Rodd Wheaton, architectural historian for the U.S. National Park Service, was encouraging from the start and offered several useful tips on sources. Erin Hannan of the Colorado Springs Fine Arts Center, and Jessy Randall and Elizabeth Smith Lewis at Colorado College's Tutt Library, were helpful in securing archival photographs. Roderick Dew, librarian at the Colorado Springs Fine Arts Center, assisted with materials on the city's arts scene.

For information on the impact of military payrolls on Colorado Springs, I am indebted to Carol Christjohn, Office of Budget and Financial Analysis, City of Colorado Springs.

Victoria Lindsay Levine, W. M. Keck Foundation director of the Hulbert Center for Southwestern Studies at Colorado College, offered early on to publish the book through the Hulbert Center Press. She and program coordinators Jim Diers and Pamela Cosel have been especially helpful in guiding me through the end stages of getting the manuscript ready for publication.

The Graham Foundation for Advanced Studies in the Fine Arts, located in Chicago, Illinois, provided an important grant for the project. This is the second grant that I have had from the Graham Foundation, and I am particularly thankful for their support, not only of this book, but of architecture-related projects around the country. In addition to providing a publisher for the book, Colorado College has made funds available for research and preparation of the manuscript: President Kathryn Mohrman through her President's Contingency Fund, Dean Richard Storey through the Russell T. Tutt Presidential Discretionary Fund, and the Hulbert Center for Southwestern Studies through its Jackson Fellowships.

Readers should note that historic homes typically are named after the original owner/client. Exceptions are made when subsequent owners occupy the house for a long period, as the Petersons have in what I now call the Wood-Peterson house. The First Vradenburg house was originally designed for William S. Roe, who had to abandon the project before it was completed. The Ingrahams redesigned the unfinished house for new owners George and Bee Vradenburg. In 1966 the architects designed a second home for the Vradenburgs.

Elaine Freed
Colorado Springs, Colorado
2003

This book is about mid-century modern houses but, having said that, I realize that "modern" is a word with many connotations but very little definition. In describing architecture, "contemporary" often substitutes for "modern," but "contemporary" could just as easily refer to any era. "Modern" tends to mean invented, rational, and deliberate. We do not think of folk objects as modern, for example. "Modern" implies new and innovative, even avant-garde, but many modern houses—those built in the first half of the twentieth century—are now historic. Fifty years is the cutoff for nominations to the National Register of Historic Places.

Modern houses have certain shared characteristics, but not all are the same. An open plan, with rooms flowing one to the other, is typical in modern houses. Most lack applied ornament, although Frank Lloyd Wright used such a variety of line and material that his house exteriors are often richly detailed and the result appears as ornament. Modern houses more often than not follow a strong horizontal composition, although some are several stories high. In modern houses materials generally are used in a straightforward manner without disguise: glass appears as glass, cement block as cement block, etc. For that reason, modern houses commonly are thought by some to look spare and cold.

Many would agree that modern houses are unconventional, which is true, especially if you do not include the common suburban ranch house as modern. Although the modern house has usually been honored within the architectural profession and has appealed to a small population of clients, the general public prefers something more traditional. Even today, neighborhoods sometimes rise up to exclude a modern house because adjacent homeowners consider it ugly and offensive. They see its differentness as negative.

To say that a house is modern does not say much, although it suggests many things. To help the reader, and myself, get past all this uncertainty, I have provided a context of modern house evolution, both in America and Europe. I have also described Frank Lloyd Wright's mid-century Usonian houses, which had an immense influence on the designs of Elizabeth and Gordon Ingraham.

The evolution of the modern house owes a great deal to developments in technology and, in fact, is very dependent on technological gains in infrastructure, building materials, and appliances. Ready access to steel, glass, concrete, and insulation changed the nature of houses in the Western world. Central heating systems and electricity, especially lighting, were essential to the open plan. Taken for granted in the twenty-first century, these amenities are surprisingly recent, as demonstrated by Merritt Ierley in *The Comforts of Home: The American House and the Evolution of Modern Convenience*. As late as 1940 only 42 percent of American households had central heating. By 1950, 64 percent had full bathrooms.[2] Electricity, which powers myriad systems and appliances in the home, was available to two-thirds of American homes by the late 1920s.[3] Architects at mid-century, therefore, were working with what still remained relatively new and experimental systems. Inventions and discoveries occurred continually. Innovative designers, striving for path-breaking solutions, were always at risk of making major errors. At the same time, they were able to take advantage of new products and processes that were simply unavailable to earlier designers.

Architects and homebuilders took advantage of other changes. During the 1930s and until 1945 construction had nearly come to a standstill, first owing to the Great Depression and then to World War II. Peace and prosperity altered the construction landscape: rationing ended and war-scarce materials gradually became available for homebuilding. Huge markets opened up as veterans returned home to start families and study under the G. I. Bill. Federal financing, begun during the depression years to help poor families with housing, expanded after the war to aid the middle class. Americans concentrated on rebuilding their lives and thinking about tomorrow.

This book focuses on the brief period after the war when the firm of Ingraham and Ingraham designed homes for young clients in Colorado Springs, Colorado. My purpose is to bring an important regional architectural firm to wider public attention. Typically, architecture schools and architectural writers recognize designers from Chicago and the two coasts. Designers from the country's interior tend to get short shrift. Yet architects like the Ingrahams created a significant body of work, closely tied to the mainstream of modernism. Their work should be known and recognized. Other Colorado modernists of note—Victor Hornbein of Denver, Fritz Benedict of Aspen, and A. Jan Ruhtenberg of Colorado Springs—warrant greater attention as well.

I have used a personal, experiential approach to the Ingrahams's early work. Both Elizabeth and Gordon had strong ties to Frank Lloyd Wright, she as Wright's granddaughter and Gordon as a Taliesin apprentice. Many questions come to mind. What difference did it make to belong to America's most noted architectural dynasty? How did it affect the work? What was it like for their young clients to commission a Wrightian house? How involved were they in the design and construction process? What has it been like to live in such a house? How have these houses stood the test of time? What have been the limits of modern houses in the marketplace?

One thing I know is true: clients who choose a talented studio architect, rather than a commercial design firm or a builder, become engaged in a close collaboration with the designer. Together they produce a functional building that also stands as a personal expression and a work of art. It's more like having a baby than buying a car. You organize your life around it; it's not just a roof over your head. Homebuyers occasionally have a disastrous relationship with an architect, but conscientious designers are attuned to their clients and serve their needs.

The costs of custom-designed houses are high and no longer affordable for middle-class prospective homeowners. The Ingrahams, who charged too little and probably spent too much time on their projects, were able to accommodate some clients of modest means, especially in their first years of practice. Perhaps a time will come when construction efficiencies and technological breakthroughs open up the custom home option to more people. In the meantime, we can appreciate what two young architects and their clients were able to accomplish in those promising days after World War II.

Chapter One

The Modern House in America

Fig. 1. Schindler/Chace house, Los Angeles, 1921-22. Architect, R. M. Schindler. An early 20th-century example of indoor/outdoor living, the Schindler/Chace house comprised four studio areas, each with its own garden court.

Fig. 2. Lovell Health House, Los Angeles, 1927–29. Architect, Richard Neutra. The Vienna-born Neutra emigrated to America in 1923 and quickly made a name for himself in California with the design of an International Style house for Dr. Philip Lovell.

In 1947 when Gordon and Elizabeth Wright Ingraham left Chicago for the West, modernist residential design was already a vital part of the American landscape and was about to take a giant leap forward. European influences shaped much of this movement, exemplified by Gerrit Rietveld's Schröder house in Holland, Alvar Aalto's Villa Mairea in Finland, and Le Corbusier's Villa Savoie outside Paris.[4] European architects followed the flow of ideas to the United States in the 1930s as Hitler's oppression of the modern forced an exodus of artists, musicians, and architects, including Herbert Bayer, Walter Gropius, Marcel Breuer, and Ludwig Mies van der Rohe. All four had taught at Germany's famous Bauhaus School, which coupled modern design with the principle of integrating the arts and crafts.[5] Rudolf M. Schindler and Richard Neutra, both trained in Vienna, had preceded the Bauhaus group to America, as had the Finnish architect Eliel Saarinen, who emigrated in 1923. Schindler left Vienna in 1914, worked in Frank Lloyd Wright's Chicago office, and then moved to Los Angeles in 1920, where he supervised construction of Wright's Barnsdall house. Schindler established an architectural office and designed many houses of note, including his own on King's Road in Hollywood. Neutra followed in 1923, first to New York and then briefly to Wisconsin with Wright before joining Schindler in 1925 in Los Angeles.[6]

In Britain, the turn-of-the-century work of Charles Rennie Mackintosh, Edwin Lutyens, and C. F. A. Voysey drew on traditional country house design along with British vernacular to create a new look of exaggerated, abstracted, stripped-down features that appeared to be at the same time startling and familiar.[7] Later, between the wars, British architects Amyas Connell, Basil Ward, and Maxwell Fry were among those who experimented with a more straightforward modern house design, often expressed in concrete.[8] Despite the considerable talent for modernism emanating from England in the 1930s, it was the continental Europeans who carried the day. The English house had always charmed Americans, but for its traditional rather than modern qualities.

The debt to European modernists was considerable, but architects in America had not been idle. Charles and Henry Greene, along with Bernard Maybeck, broke new ground in California early in the twentieth century. Irving Gill, also in California, designed stark white, rectilinear houses with a muted salute to the region's Spanish mission past.[9] Frank Lloyd Wright experimented with customized concrete block, designing several homes in Los Angeles. Southern California, with its lush landscapes, salubrious climate, and sense of cultural destiny, offered a perfect environment for the modern house.

Europe and America dominated modern house design for good reason. New ideas about living—informality, privacy, intimacy, comfort, family life—had been taking form since the seventeenth century, but it was technological invention that greased the wheels of modernism in the twentieth century to create a new kind of house and a new sense of home.[10] Central heating and electricity, two of the most significant changes, enabled residents to enter and use any rooms of their choosing, day or night. The open plan, so important to modern house design, required ready heat and light for comfort's sake and convenience as well. A century earlier, the entire family had gathered around a kitchen range or parlor stove, reading under a fuel lamp or by candlelight, while the rest of the house stood dark, cold, and empty.[11]

At the close of the nineteenth century, Frank Lloyd Wright built a bridge from the old era to the new, incorporating technical advances and advocating new ways to live. Wright argued for informality and greater simplicity. His midwestern Prairie houses from that period offered alternatives to tradition. The asymmetrical exteriors, bands of windows, horizontal lines, and great eaves were precursors to his later work.[12] Wright's modern designs evolved for another sixty years until his death in 1959 and included the revolutionary Usonian house that was to have enormous influence on the postwar work of Elizabeth and Gordon Ingraham.[13]

Frank Lloyd Wright was nearly seventy in 1937 when he designed his first Usonian house, a modest dwelling for the Herbert Jacobs family in Madison, Wisconsin. By that time, after so many years of life and work, he had developed firm principles about domestic design, which he offered up to the reader of his book, *The Natural House*, as a set of "do's" and "don'ts":

Do	Don't
Flat or slant roof	Pitched roof, attic
Carport	Garage
Slab foundation	Basement
Plasticity, natural materials	Applied ornament
Gravity heat from floor level	Radiators
Indirect lighting	Light fixtures
Built-in storage and furniture	Movable furniture
Oil finish on redwood	Paint
Brick, wood, and glass interiors	Plaster
Overhanging eaves	Gutters, downspouts[14]

This cheat sheet for constructing the "natural house" does not exhaust Wright's prescriptions by any means. He strived for a result that expressed simplicity, not plainness, and therefore he disliked the work of his contemporary, Gustav Stickley, and other exemplars of the severe Mission styles.[15] His requirement for simplicity did not preclude graciousness. He went so far as to chide people for not knowing how to live and for being full of prejudices misinterpreted as tastes.[16] He believed people were too ready to imitate grand mansions down the block rather than reach within themselves to express their own needs and aspirations. Wright's very successful attempts to combine simplicity with flair and drama were emulated later by Gordon and Elizabeth Ingraham and many of his former apprentices.

Wright was genuinely excited about the possibilities of technology and the proliferation of accessible, affordable man-made materials that would enhance the modern house. His talk of organic architecture and natural materials sometimes misleads—one thinks of mushroom shapes rising out of the ground with only stone and wood allowed into the process. On the contrary, he knew that steel, with its option of

Fig. 3.
Villa Savoie, Poissy,
France, 1929. Architect,
Le Corbusier. An early
proponent of what
became known as the
International Style, Le
Corbusier created new
house forms as
machines for living.

cantilever, could alter both the look and function of a house. He recognized that glass could revolutionize interior lighting and could also blur the line between inside and outside, thus adding greatly to the notion of an integrated house.[17] Residents would see in a different way, the sky would become a daily feature of indoor life. "You may see that walls are vanishing," he said, noting that humans at last were moving out of the cave.[18]

Although Wright expressed patronizing comments about his women clients, he recognized that the mid-century, servantless, affordable house must be planned to accommodate women who were cooking, cleaning, raising children, and perhaps trying to do work of their own.[19] He touted the open plan, where children could be seen from many vantage points, both inside and out, and began substituting the word "workspace" for kitchen, perhaps in an effort to elevate and broaden the functions of that room.[20]

The 1937 Jacobs house in Madison, Wisconsin, accommodated mother, father, a son and a daughter—the quintessential twentieth-century American family. By that time Wright's own domestic situation was far from the norm—in 1932 he and his third wife, Olgivanna, had started the Taliesin Fellowship, a school for architecture and arts that was organized as a commune.[21] But he continued to design single-family houses and to worry about the seemingly insoluble problem of producing distinctive, personalized houses that would match the limited budgets of most Americans.[22]

In 1974 British architect and scholar John Sergeant published a survey of Frank Lloyd Wright's Usonian houses. He analyzed their unusual construction and innovative technologies. He observed the cultural context at mid-century that made Usonian houses appealing. Americans liked the efficiencies in a modern house, and Wright's popularity—or better yet, celebrity—encouraged middle-class prospective clients to take the leap toward innovative design.[23] Sergeant reiterates Wright's solutions: how he moved away from the formal dining room, which had once been central to his homes, and

Fig. 4.
Jacobs house, Madison, Wisconsin, 1937. Architect Frank Lloyd Wright. Salient features of this landmark house—brick fireplace, clerestory windows, horizontal wooden paneling, and built-in cabinetry—appeared later in homes designed by Ingraham and Ingraham.

Fig. 5.
Jacobs house, Madison, Wisconsin, 1937. Architect, Frank Lloyd Wright. Wright's first Usonian house, designed on a modest scale and at a low cost, established Wright as an innovator in high-style, affordable housing.

placed the kitchen, or workspace, at the center of activity instead; and how he placed kitchen and bath in a service core that increased the economy of heating and plumbing. Sergeant also details Wright's Usonian planning grids: "The dimensions of board and batten gave a regular 'stripe' or vertical module of 1 foot 1 inch, and this controlled the height of window transoms, sills, the 'decks' for concealed lighting, bookshelves, eaves, clerestory windows, and chimneys."[24] Wright used a horizontal two-foot-by-four-foot module on the floor plan. These grids made designing more rational and efficient and helped contractors identify how features and materials should be placed.[25]

Sergeant, who visited Wright's Usonians—and their owners—throughout the 1960s and early 1970s, confirmed that owners were satisfied with Wright's principles and design solutions. Overall, they found the houses to be serene, harmonious, and secure.[26] They liked the counterpoint of openness, as in the living or public areas, and privacy, as in the bedroom wings. Clients approved of Wright's application of human scale, which he somehow managed to combine with an impression of spaciousness, and they liked the practical aspects of floor-based gravity heat.[27] Conversely, some owners complained about the small kitchens, especially those built without windows in the core of the house, and the lack of play area for children, who as a result tended to take over the living room.[28] Ingraham clients, wholly or in part because of finances, experienced these limitations as well.

Gordon Ingraham learned directly about Wright's work in 1940 when he spent roughly a year with the Taliesin Fellowship, first in Wisconsin and then Arizona.[29] Elizabeth grew up around and within Wright designs and then saw many of the same principles applied by her architect father, John Lloyd Wright. Her uncle, architect Lloyd Wright, introduced Elizabeth to the work of California architects Irving Gill and R. M. Schindler during her year at Berkeley in 1939-40.[30] Both Ingrahams would have seen some of Wright's Prairie houses, his early work from roughly 1890 to 1910, and they would have known about Fallingwater and Wingspread, two of Wright's grandest houses from the 1930s. They would have been intimately knowledgeable about the great house at Taliesin in Wisconsin and the newer complex at Taliesin West in Scottsdale, Arizona. They would have visited the Jacobs house in Madison, Wisconsin, as well as any number of Usonians realized by Wright in the 1940s. By the time he reissued *The Natural House* in 1954, Wright reported more than 100 Usonian houses already built around the country.[31] The Ingrahams viewed much of Wright's work firsthand and they also learned about Wright's houses from the press. His work was well publicized in contemporary shelter magazines.[32]

Given the Ingrahams's strong personal ties to Wright, it is no wonder they were enthralled by his design work and philosophy. Their own training and early professional work reinforced those early influences, particularly as they got underway in Chicago during the war years.

Chicago in the 1940s more than any other experience shaped the Ingrahams's aesthetic and design principles. Elizabeth recalls the period as contentious and vivid: "Studying with Mies during 1940-42, I was in the architectural crowd where the hot debate on Mies versus Wright raged—Ralph Rapson, Harry Weese, Kevin Lynch, the start of SOM [the firm of Skidmore, Owings and Merrill] with Nat Owings, Louis Skidmore, and John Merrill and also Moholy-Nagy and the rest of the Bauhaus crowd."[33] The Ingrahams married in 1944 and returned to Chicago after the war to work for William Deknatel. The sense of Chicago's vitality stayed with Elizabeth throughout her life: "I have

Fig. 6. Taliesin, Spring Green, Wisconsin. Frank Lloyd Wright's famous living room, photographed here by Pedro Guerrero about 1940, inspired architects to break out of the box.

never seen any other time that so epitomized America at its best ... innovative, challenged, productive, caught in the great surge of energy that drove us after World War II."[34]

The Ingrahams respected Richard Neutra's and Harwell Hamilton Harris's California work and admired Victor Hornbein, who was in Denver. The Europeans captured their interest: "We related to Eliel Saarinen and thought highly of him, particularly his work at Cranbrook [Cranbrook Academy in Michigan]."[35] Elizabeth thought highly of the German architect Erich Mendelsohn as well, especially his work in the Middle East, and she maintained a lifelong interest in architect Louis Kahn. The Ingrahams admired Albert Kahn, who became famous as a designer for the Detroit automotive industry. But not every modernist appealed to them. "I inherited my dislike of Gropius from my grandfather and never seemed to change it; however, I did like Marcel Breuer and certainly Alvar Aalto."[36] Elizabeth sensed that Le Corbusier, the Swiss-born modern architect and painter, was not as big a force in Chicago as he was at that time in the East.

Although both Wright and Chicago had laid claim to the Ingrahams's sensibilities, the couple was eager to try life and work in the West, which seemed a welcoming environment for new ideas, and proved to be so.[37] Concurrent with the Ingrahams's early work in Colorado, developer Edward Hawkins was creating a modernist subdivision in south Denver, using both Frank Lloyd Wright and Mies van der Rohe as inspiration for design.

Fig. 7. Taliesin, Spring Green, Wisconsin, 1911, 1914, 1925, and on-going. Architect, Frank Lloyd Wright. For Wright, Taliesin's bucolic setting set the stage for the architect's home and studio: surrounding farmland testified to life-giving agriculture and healthy community. Wright himself was more country squire than farmer.

The thirty-acre development accommodated 124 houses, sited to ensure variety and privacy. Hawkins hired Eugene Sternberg, a Czech-born architect trained at Cambridge University, who had recently joined the faculty of Denver University's new School of Architecture and Planning. He was influenced by Marcel Breuer, who had taught at the Bauhaus in Germany. After the project's first year, Hawkins assumed the design process himself, assisted by Joseph Dion. According to Diane Wray in *Arapahoe Acres: An Architectural History 1949-1957*, Hawkins's tastes leaned heavily towards Wright's Usonian, and it became the model for Arapahoe Acres after an early smattering of International Style homes.[38] Prospective homeowners flocked to the subdivision in early 1950 to see the new materials and construction innovations that Hawkins and his team offered—and at reasonable prices, beginning at $10,000. Wray notes that Hawkins "was a charismatic individual who inspired great loyalty."[39] He assumed responsibility for educating homebuyers and insisted that they follow his design tastes. Wray describes the quintessential Hawkins/Sternberg product: "Exterior construction materials expanded to include natural stone, concrete block, a wide variety of brick, tongue and groove siding, board and batten siding and lapboard siding, roof and balcony fascia. Wood sunscreens, louvers and other details appeared. Glass became an important exterior design element."[40] In other words, these flat-roofed modernist Denver homes might have been Ingraham designs, so close were they to the Usonian requirements set out by Frank Lloyd Wright, even to the gravity heat systems buried in the slab foundations.

California, which offered fertile ground for modern design in the first half of the twentieth century, continued to attract innovative architects and developers after World War II. Although the Ingrahams were not drawn to California as a home base, they were attuned to its modern design history and postwar vitality. They followed the new work. Beginning in the early 1950s, developer Joseph Eichler built 10,000 modernist houses in the Palo Alto area of California, using a team of ranking area architects, including Robert Anshen, Steven Allen, A. Quincy Jones, Frederick Emmons, and later the firm of Claude Oakland & Associates. Rather than relying on site engineers, Eichler hired architects to design the site plans using curved streets and cul-de-sacs. Eichler, too, had become a Frank Lloyd Wright follower. He and his young family rented a Wright house for a brief period in the 1940s and the experience made a lasting impression. He was easily persuaded to adopt a modernist approach to his California designs. In addition to incorporating Wrightian and International Style innovations, he soon made news by adding a second bathroom to his houses—a rarity then in modestly priced homes—and an atrium. To keep up, other developers began including these "luxury" features. Like Denver developer Edward Hawkins, Joseph Eichler was a charismatic, aggressive promoter whose enthusiasm for modernism persuaded thousands of home-buying prospects to share his tastes.[41]

Fig. 8. Design studio at Taliesin West, Scottsdale, Arizona, 1939. Architect, Frank Lloyd Wright. Wright's bold new forms at Taliesin West were born of necessity: architectural commissions fell off during the Great Depression. His low-cost "desert masonry" incorporated fieldstone from the surrounding foothills.

California had in fact been home to innovative design since early in the twentieth century. Greene and Greene, Irving Gill, Frank Lloyd Wright, R. M. Schindler, and Richard Neutra brought new forms and materials to California clients and set the stage for a postwar surge of modernist design, a movement energized and directed by John Entenza, editor of *Arts and Architecture* magazine in Los Angeles. Entenza helped create the mood of architectural change and optimism in the West that triggered Gordon and Elizabeth Ingrahams's decision to settle there. In 1945 he launched a project to hire eight architectural firms to design eight houses—the magazine would be the client. Named the Case Study program, Entenza's unique project resulted in thirteen new houses in the first five years. They tilted more towards Mies than Wright and became a proving ground for the use of steel in residential design. Not only were experimental houses built, they were publicized widely and exerted a huge influence. In *Case Study Houses 1945–1962*, Esther McCoy describes the impact: "Soon after the end of the war the editorial offices of the magazine had become a virtual clearing house for architectural information in the Los Angeles area, with Entenza acting as an orientation committee for visiting editors and critics."[42]

Entenza was not alone in his editorializing modernist mission. On the East Coast, the Museum of Modern Art (MoMA) led a similar charge by publishing books and manuals on how to build modern, live modern, be modern. In 1946, just as Entenza was proselytizing the Case Study houses, and just as Elizabeth and Gordon Ingraham were first starting to consider a move from Chicago to the West, MoMA issued Elizabeth Mock's *If You Want to Build a House*, a guide for the postwar generation on how to kick off the old traces and enter the world of modern architecture. Mock uses simple, straightforward language to persuade her readers that hiring an architect—and specifically hiring a modern architect—is not a scary prospect, but rather a sensible, satisfying, and responsible act that will result in a better and happier life for the client. This small book—fewer than 100 pages, generously illustrated with 120 black-and-white photographs—makes a case for a Wrightian look along Usonian lines (among the photographs are seventeen examples of Wright's houses). Like Wright, Mock promotes individualism as the highest organizing principle for living: "Remember that your family is made up of highly differentiated individuals, each eager to pursue his life under the pleasantest circumstances and with a minimum of interference. This means that the real basis for house-planning should be the individual, not the group."[43]

Mock criticized the futuristic Streamline Art Deco and Moderne houses popular in the 1930s and 1940s as too stark, too stylized. Describing kitchens from that era, she complains of their "antiseptic meagerness,"[44] and later she speaks of "the instinctive dislike of slick surfaces."[45] Implicit is her disapproval of the International Style practiced by Mies van der Rohe and Le Corbusier, which would be considered overly formal, impersonal, and much too Spartan. For Mock at MoMA and for many other promulgators of innovative design, some modernism was better than others. She clearly comes down on the side of the warmer, more expressive, more organic designs of the Wrightian school. Other influential writers of the period made the same choice. Elizabeth Gordon, editor of *House Beautiful*, promoted Wright for nearly two decades and waged war against the internationalists.[46]

Modernist architectural writers and editors, whether they favored Mies or Wright, adopted the "brave-new-world tone" described by Esther McCoy in recalling John Entenza's Case Study program.[47] McCoy characterizes the 1940s as "a period with a strong social conscience, a reflection of the idealism and puritanism of the depression

Fig. 9.
Case Study House #22,
Los Angeles, 1959.
Architect, Pierre Koenig.
When Koenig designed
this dramatic steel-
framed house as part of
magazine editor John
Entenza's California
competition, he was
continuing an
approach begun in
1950 while still a student
at the University of
Southern California.
Julius Shulman's famous
photographs made the
house a modernist icon.

and war years when architecture was first of all a social art."[48] The mood was serious but optimistic. Scarcity, a by-product of both the depression and the war, challenged builders and designers to make the most of available materials. Many architects accepted the challenge, designing small, inexpensive houses that managed at the same time to offer clients a bold and efficient use of space. The descriptive language for the process balances innovation and risk on the one hand with realism and responsibility on the other.

A 1953 survey of modern houses captures the intent and tone used by contemporary writers. The survey, by Jean and Don Graf, entitled *Practical Houses for Living*, describes thirty-nine recently designed and constructed American homes. Not all clients' professions are noted, but of the thirty-nine, ten were designed by architects to live in themselves. Five clients were medical doctors, one was a judge, another a paint company president, and several were described as teachers, writers, and artists—in short, well educated and middle class or higher. An architect-designed house was probably a financial stretch for some members of this audience. The book of plans and photographs carries the "practical house" theme throughout. A few of the houses are high-end with such amenities as a maid's room and a swimming pool, but most were exercises in sensible choices: "A traveled lady settles down—and chooses modern that is easy to keep neat."[49] The authors summarize their offerings: "Ingenuity, hard-headed practicality and a fine regard for the personal element characterize these houses."[50] Like Elizabeth Mock in the MoMA guide, the Grafs try to persuade readers that a custom-designed house is within their reach and, unlike a tract house, will express their individuality and tastes. Even Frank Lloyd Wright, designer of dramatic and bold homes for wealthy clients, used the language of practicality: "What would be really sensible in this matter of the modest dwelling for our time and place? Let's see how far the first

Fig. 10.
Denver house, 1938. Architects around the country designed Streamline Art Deco and Moderne styles throughout the 1930s, which kept modernism in the public eye, even though traditional styles continued to dominate popular tastes. In any case, America's entry into World War II in 1941 brought most home construction to a halt.

Herbert Jacobs house in Madison, Wisconsin, is a sensible house."[51] He then goes on to cite the home's low cost—$5,500 in 1937—and urges like-minded prospective clients to simplify their lives and get down to essentials. For imaginative, disciplined clients, vision trumped money.

This language of aspiration, combined with a Spartan ideal, resonated with the fledgling firm of Ingraham and Ingraham, willing to show the way to its Western clients. Hundreds of young architects all over the country were moving in the same modernist direction, and a significant number of prospective homeowners were prepared to follow them. Yet, tradition dies hard, especially in matters residential. Conservative tastes maintained their currency, and developers understood well how to marry the building boom to familiar choices. Cape Cod cottages and ranch houses dominated the landscape from coast to coast, despite the efforts of architectural schools, designers, and much of the press to create a home for the modern. The numbers are telling: The Ingrahams designed and built fifteen houses in their first five years of practice in Colorado Springs, an impressive record of work. But before they even got started, developer John Bonforte had already completed nearly 300 crackerbox houses in the Bonnyville neighborhood.[52] It was the same everywhere. Looking back on the Entenza years in California, writer Esther McCoy summed it up: "By 1960 the custom-built family small house was being priced out of existence... By 1962 it had become clear that the battle for housing had been won by the developers, with more drafting services involved than architects. Housing was a gigantic industry, and the cost of land and construction was of greater concern to the builders than good environment."[53]

Fig. 11. Denver house, 1937. Postwar architects might have considered the 1930s styles slightly dated, but the presence of earlier modern house styles would have offered encouragement to firms like the Ingrahams's.

The Ingrahams designed thirty-five houses and eight institutional and commercial buildings during twenty-two years of practice together. In addition, they accomplished a large number of additions and remodelings. They began their work in the late 1940s with a stunning clarity of vision and great energy. Arguably they created their best work at the outset for a handful of like-minded clients in Colorado Springs. Although their work constituted only a small fraction of the city's built environment, it captured and exemplified an important segment of the American dream.

Chapter Two

The Move to Colorado

A 10,000 mile automobile tour of the West in 1947 left the Ingrahams convinced that Colorado Springs should be their home—it seemed the right place at the right time. Here was a town on the move in the expanding West, but still small enough to feel like a community. Always a prosperous, privileged place, the city—with a population of 45,000 in 1949—offered spectacular views and easy access to both mountains and plains. The art scene was lively. With only a handful of architects in practice, there seemed plenty of room for two transplanted Chicagoans eager to bring modernist ideas to the frontier. The Ingrahams shared, if not an active aversion to urban life, a Wrightian belief that a pastoral setting was to be preferred over the city.[54]

The Ingrahams's choice of Colorado Springs proved fortunate in some respects and ill starred in others. The city offered a superior context for exercising their talents as residential designers—within five years they had designed more than fifteen houses, all but one in Colorado. It was a remarkable body of work and remains so a half-century later. But despite their energies and aspirations, the Ingrahams never successfully tapped the huge market for commercial and institutional buildings that soon grew up in and around the city. They created an important niche early on and established a creditable practice, but the going got tougher after their initial success. Even before they had settled themselves in Colorado Springs, the city had begun its move toward spiraling growth that was heavily invested in the military—a good fit neither with the Ingraham aesthetic nor their social values. Further, they never successfully mastered marketing. Depending too much on word of mouth for clients, they were slow to develop a client base. Personal problems also came into play: a contentious marriage spilled over into the practice, and Gordon's drinking compromised his work. The Ingrahams eventually divorced and then dissolved the firm. Finally, modernism—their forte—began to fade by the end of the sixties. Traditional houses had always been popular and with the growing strength of the historic preservation movement, older homes attracted the small clientele that might earlier have chosen a modern house. These problems and constraints, so easy to identify in hindsight, remained hidden for some years. At the outset, as the Ingrahams established themselves in the West, they envisioned a very bright future.

Both Gordon and Elizabeth Ingraham arrived in Colorado Springs with excellent, even enviable, training and connections. Gordon had graduated from the University of Virginia with a degree in architecture, followed by a year at Frank Lloyd Wright's Taliesin and entry-level jobs in Chicago working for William Deknatel, George Fred Keck, and then Skidmore, Owings and Merrill. Elizabeth, the daughter of architect John Lloyd Wright and granddaughter of famed Frank Lloyd Wright, had design in her blood and bones from the start. (When she announced in her late teens that she intended to become an architect, her mother replied: "How original.")[55] Elizabeth apprenticed with Mies van der Rohe, then director of the School of Architecture of the Illinois Institute of

Fig. 12. Residence of Victor Hornbein, Denver, 1948. Architect, Victor Hornbein. Hornbein admired Frank Lloyd Wright's work and was influenced by him. Hornbein and his wife welcomed the Ingrahams to Colorado, albeit with some caveats, and remained lifelong friends.

Technology. Along with Gordon she worked with Deknatel in Chicago, and later took jobs there with Morgan Yost and Paul Schweikher.

When they first came to Colorado, the Ingrahams accepted an invitation from architect Fritz Benedict in Aspen to help him with projects there. Benedict and Gordon were at Taliesin together in 1940. Benedict was teamed in Aspen with Herbert Bayer, an extraordinary Bauhaus designer who loomed very large in that small Colorado mountain town and who, at mid-century, could claim a first-rank place in both American and European design.

Aspen was just beginning its postwar ascent. The Ingrahams were impressed but not tempted to stay. They felt uneasy in Aspen. Gordon summed up their reaction: "We were conservative in that we felt we should begin in a more stable environment. We had very little money. Then, too, we felt pressed by the mountains, strange but true. Perhaps we felt that we were in a cul-de-sac that might have no further horizons."[56] They admired the efforts of Walter and Elizabeth Paepcke, who developed Aspen as a cultural mecca, but ultimately the Ingrahams found the place confining.

A colleague in Denver, fellow modernist Victor Hornbein, had suggested Colorado Springs. On their way west, the Ingrahams stopped in Denver to meet Hornbein. They liked his work, which was close to the familiar Wright idiom. Hornbein and his wife, Ruth, coupled their recommendation of Colorado Springs with cautionary remarks. Victor described it as a tourist town, sleepy in winter but in a beautiful setting. "I don't know much about the chances of you getting clients to support you."[57] Ruth concurred, saying Colorado Springs was slow to accept new ideas. She added that Denver was bad enough on that score.

Elizabeth later recalled the Ingrahams's puzzlement over the apparent lack of interest, or understanding, shown by the Western building industry for regional environmental issues. "Harsh bright sunlight, generally dry conditions, high winds. These prevail over the entire area and yet people use forms and materials from the East. This made no sense to us."[58] They talked about their concerns early on with local ranchers, but at the time no one seemed to care.

During a scouting visit to Colorado Springs, the Ingrahams met Douglas Jardine, a prominent plumbing and heating contractor, who encouraged them to start a practice. They were trying to determine whether a new architectural firm would have much opportunity. Jardine suggested they visit with John Bonforte, who was developing a residential subdivision two miles north of downtown. There were lots of identical little houses lined up in a row in Bonforte's new complex, not an aesthetic inspiration for the Ingrahams although they viewed the development as much-needed affordable housing. The degree to which developers would dominate the building industry was not yet evident. All in all, the Ingrahams were impressed with the region's potential for design, building, and growth. "Alas," Gordon said forty years later, "we never did ask anyone concerning the political frame that existed then. Much the same as it is now. Highly Republican and very conservative."[59]

On arrival in Pikes Peak country they immediately discovered a compatible group of intellectuals and artists who became close friends and, in some instances, clients: painters Lewis and Martha Tilley, Herman Raymond, Bishop Nash, Vincent and Ellen O'Brien, Archie and Irene Musick, and Eric and Marianne Bransby. Other artists were Edgar and Margaret Britton (a sculptor and ceramicist), Guy and Lorraine Burgess (photographer and writer), George and Lillian McCue (professor of literature and writer). These artists and others like them hovered around three important cultural institutions: Fountain Valley School, a boarding school founded in 1930; Colorado College, a long-established liberal arts college; and the Colorado Springs Fine Arts Center, newly minted in 1936. In a town of 45,000, these three operations commanded respect and attention. With such rich resources, artists were regularly commissioned to do work and to teach and exhibit.[60]

Other talented newcomers joined their ranks. In 1948, musicians Henry and Irene Margolinski, moved to Colorado Springs from China. He had been conductor of the Shanghai Symphony until the communist takeover of mainland China. She was a concert pianist, and both became active in the city's musical world. By then, impresario Carol Truax had taken over the college's art and music departments and brought to campus composer Roy Harris and, in residence, the LaSalle String Quartet. Virgil Thomson and Paul Hindemith were among the musical luminaries whom Truax attracted during the college's summer sessions. New York modern dance choreographer Hanya Holm also began her long summer session career in the 1940s as a performer and dance teacher.[61] A. Jan Ruhtenberg, a noted modernist architect trained at the Bauhaus, had emigrated to America in 1933 and moved to Colorado Springs a few years later, where he designed avant-garde homes in the International Style. These creative music and design artists added further underpinning to the city's reputation in the late 1940s as a sophisticated art colony.

Three local, wealthy art patrons had done much to set the stage: Julie Penrose, Alice Bemis Taylor, and Elizabeth Sage Hare. All three had strong ties to the Taos and Santa Fe art scenes, and all three put their energies and money into the Broadmoor Art Academy and its later incarnation as the Colorado Springs Fine Arts Center. In 1919, Julie Penrose, wife of hotelier, developer, and mining baron Spencer Penrose, donated land and her home to house the Broadmoor Art Academy and a gallery. In the mid-1930s, Alice Bemis Taylor hired John Gaw Meem to design a new arts center on the Penrose site to hold her huge collection of Indian and Spanish arts and crafts. As plans for the building progressed, Taylor was persuaded to make the museum a true center for the arts, including drama, dance, music, film, and art studio.[62]

In the meantime, Elizabeth Sage Hare, who moved to Colorado from New York in 1928, recruited nationally known and professionally trained artists to work and teach at both Fountain Valley School and the art academy. These included Boardman Robinson, a superb draftsman and ranking realist who had taught at the Art Students League in New York. Hare also staged an avant-garde opening for the arts center in 1936 that introduced Colorado Springs to the latest in European and New York performance and art, featuring Martha Graham's dance company and Erik Satie's symphony drama, *Socrate*.

Boardman Robinson headed up the old Broadmoor Art Academy and was then appointed as director of the new Fine Arts Center school.[63] Robinson had impressive credentials. He had become a prolific and accomplished magazine illustrator, serving for example as art editor at *Vogue* in New York and as a cartoonist for *The Masses*. Edgar Kaufmann, owner of Frank Lloyd Wright's Fallingwater, had commissioned Robinson in 1927 to create a mural series entitled "History of Commerce" for Kaufmann's Pittsburgh department store.[64] As a populist and socialist, Robinson horrified local conservatives early on but apparently gained acceptance, thanks to the bona fides of his privileged sponsors. Eric Bransby, a Colorado Springs muralist, believed that Robinson set a standard for the region's artists. As head of the art school, he attracted promising, talented students from around the country.

Signs of change in the city appeared near mid-century, about the time the Ingrahams came to town. In 1947, Boardman Robinson resigned his post at the Fine Arts Center and moved back to New York.[65] By 1949, patrons Alice Bemis Taylor and Elizabeth Sage Hare were both deceased. Julie Penrose lived until 1956 and kept the art scene always in her sights. An energetic, cosmopolitan woman, she recognized the value of the high-stepping bohemian artist crowd and acted as their liaison with the stodgier, more conservative local community. She brought the artists and local elites together at parties and continued to fund artistic programs throughout the city.

In some respects, the city's arts culture at mid-century had never been stronger. News of dance and drama productions, concerts, and exhibitions filled the local newspapers. Arts cognoscenti around the country knew of the city's cultural offerings, which were of a piece with the artists' colonies in Taos and Santa Fe. Martha Tilley, an artist of the period and an Ingraham client, believed it was a special time for the arts, a time of tremendous synergy and optimism. "I think artists never again achieved the kind of creativity of those years. Their work was never the same."[66] It was this environment of creativity that attracted and impressed the Ingrahams. Why did it change?

Several factors made the difference: first, new leadership at the Fine Arts Center shifted the institution's direction. By the late 1940s, rising operational costs outstripped

Fig. 13. Colorado Springs Fine Arts Center, Colorado Springs, Colorado, 1936. Architect, John Gaw Meem. Photographer: Laura Gilpin, ca. 1938. The new museum strengthened the city's reputation as a lively and important Western art colony.

Alice Bemis Taylor's endowment support of the arts center. Enrollments fell in the art school, especially among veterans returning from service in World War II. Director Mitchell A. Wilder sought a collaboration with the center's next-door neighbor, Colorado College, which would guarantee a steady stream of undergraduates in art studio courses.[67] In the process, the art school was subsumed under the college's aegis and its instructors held faculty status. Wilder described the shift: "Before the War the emphasis was on the full-time art student of advanced status. Today, the Colorado College undergraduates compose three-fourths of the student body."[68] Existing arts center faculty, lithographer Lawrence Barrett among them, were let go.[69] Lew Tilley, a painting instructor, was given a leave of absence.[70] Barrett appeared at a Fine Arts Center members' meeting to protest his firing and to demand an explanation.[71] Although the disputed new directions were arguably prudent and necessary, the change removed the center's art school from the ranks of national institutions that specialized in professional art training.

Fig. 14. Military parade marching south on Tejon Street in front of Busy Corner Drugs, early 1950s. The city's growing military presence increased construction throughout the region and brought with it a boom-town mentality.

The turn toward liberal arts education coincided with a shift away from an elitist art museum and a move in the direction of a broad-based community center. The highbrow versus middlebrow choice was faced by all cultural institutions of the era and remained a hot issue throughout the century. Boards of trustees saw a broader appeal as a way to increase memberships, pay the bills, and play a more comfortable role within their communities. They opened the doors, eschewing avant-garde art as complicated, off-putting, and undemocratic. They took seriously an expressed mission of educating and embracing the larger public. It was all right to exhibit serious art as long as a lot of other, more pleasing offerings brought in new visitors. In the process, museums gained access to public funds. Foundations encouraged these trends by rewarding institutions for "audience building." At the same time, the artistic experience became more accessible but arguably less interesting or valuable. Both art and its public moved towards the comfortable center.

Director Mitchell Wilder sensed other changes in the wind. By 1952, when he hired Emerson Woelffer to head the art school, the international art world had moved from realism to abstract expressionism. Realists such as Boardman Robinson suddenly seemed old fashioned and out of step. Woelffer's nonobjective paintings, on the other hand, were fresh and of the moment. By most accounts, Wilder's sweeping changes rescued the ailing art school and brought the whole operation into the new wave of artistic expression.[72]

In 1948 the Ingrahams saw only the accomplishments, the optimism, the dynamic energy of both art and artist. Their early work—powerful and rigorous—mirrored the local arts world in which they moved and from which they sought inspiration and vindication. There was no way for them to know that their first houses were in fact a capstone of a singularly auspicious era for the arts in Colorado Springs. Another world—and a very different one—was in the making.

The Fine Arts Center, in fact, proved an exemplary microcosm of the community. As the center grew larger, more diverse, and more middlebrow in the early 1950s, so did the city. Always a tourist mecca and at one time a gold mining capital and refuge for tuberculosis sufferers, some of them very wealthy, Colorado Springs had limped through the Great Depression with its old families still very much in control. World War II brought thousands of troops to Camp Carson, south of town. Business leaders, quick to see the economic benefits of a federal payroll, began a strategic campaign to bring in more military and defense agencies. Led by the Chamber of Commerce, the business community lobbied for the Air Force Academy and a regional office of the Atomic Energy Commission.[73] By late 1949, Colorado Springs was one of twenty-seven cities still in the running for the academy site, and it eventually won.[74] The city's boosters succeeded in making Camp Carson a permanent fort.[75] To service a big surge in population, the city contracted for water from Colorado's western slope, across the Continental Divide.[76]

The same newspaper that advertised an exhibition opening at the Fine Arts Center or a concert at Colorado College ran front-page reports of defense activities designed to fight the Cold War. Communists were taking over in China, the Russians had the A-bomb, flying saucers were spotted in New Mexico.[77] Even as they planned for postwar prosperity, Americans felt anxious. President Truman and Congress prepared for the worst, and those preparations included military installations, many of them in the West—and some of them in Colorado.

Securing these federal plums required a tenacious civilian army of boosters to organize and persuade Congress that Colorado Springs was the perfect place for defense spending. Before the war, the city's old families had been content to rule within a privileged but contained environment. The new entrepreneurs sought growth and fielded a cadre of lobbyists to compete for federal dollars. Their success meant more people and bigger payrolls.

Before long the city took on a new tone. The Chamber of Commerce developed a promising farm team, the Junior Chamber, and regularly recognized them for their promotional skills.[78] Service clubs, traditionally a reservoir of main-street boosterism, lent their energies to making Colorado Springs home to federal projects. A relentless optimism ruled. Despite this considerable transformation, Colorado Springs remained as conservative as ever, but instead of dour New England clergymen in charge, a group of well-connected Republican businessmen ran the town. H. Chase Stone, a banker baron with strong ties to El Pomar Foundation, was credited with commanding the federal facility blitz during the 1950s. The reigning group railed against big government even as they secured one U.S. agency after another until, by 1970, the region's economy was dependent on government for nearly half of its payroll.[79]

The wealthy old guard, sons and daughters of Cripple Creek gold wealth or descendents of earlier New England bluebloods, mingled with the newly minted rich and mostly kept their sense of superiority and disapproval to themselves. John Hazlehurst, whose grandfather Francis Drexel Smith helped shape the Broadmoor Art Academy, remembers his mother noting that H. Chase Stone was nothing more than "Babbitt in a good suit."[80] The new titans, in turn, called the old guard "troglodytes."

New buildings marked the city's growth—houses by the hundreds, and schools, shopping centers, banks, business blocks, churches—and created a demand for architects and an even greater demand for contractors and developers. A small design shop like Ingraham and Ingraham was not set up to compete at this high-stakes level. Nor did their aesthetic inclinations and client-centered practices lend themselves to large-scale, generic projects. The Ingrahams continued to concentrate on homes and other small structures, turning again and again to the science professionals and art-related clients who had supported them in the first place.

This is not to say that the city's arts world declined as the city changed. The Fine Arts Center continued to expand and prosper, the city's symphony developed a professional orchestra, Fountain Valley School and Colorado College retained their fine reputations, artists by the hundreds continued to paint and sculpt, theatre and dance groups established subscription seasons. These accomplishments were appropriate to a community reaching for the half-million mark in population. But never again in the ensuing half-century would there be the insouciance and bravado that existed among those happy few who banded together for the arts in the late 1940s, creating a brief but exuberant Golden Age. And never again was the context as compatible for creative designers like Gordon and Elizabeth Ingraham.

At a time when local forces for change—especially population growth and the ascendence of a middlebrow aesthetic—moved the city toward more traditional housing, national pressures created a similar effect. Modern design, so full of promise at the end of World War II, was losing its hold on American tastemakers at the end of the 1960s. From a hemisphere away, the war in Vietnam was turning this country upside down. Deyan Sudjic, writing in *Home: The Twentieth-Century House*, describes the change: "The fundamental optimism that had underpinned architectural modernity into the 1960s evaporated."[81] Clients no longer sought a high-tech look. Developers, sensing as well as shaping change, replaced the popular ranch house with eclectic historic styles. Tastes shifted toward rustic, indigenous forms that used logs and rough planks. In Colorado, the ski-lodge look adapted from nineteenth-century mining sheds became the vogue. The modern movement would live to fight another day, but for the moment it receded in the landscape. Frank Lloyd Wright and Mies van der Rohe—once such powerful figures in American design—became, in effect, homeless.

Chapter Three

The Work, The Family

The Ingrahams began their practice as many professionals do, with clients drawn from among their social circle and new acquaintances. From the beginning they formed a strong attachment to artists and teachers at the Fine Arts Center, Fountain Valley School, and Colorado College. John Fundingsland, an inventor and Colorado College music professor, walked into the Ingrahams's new studio on Cascade Avenue early in 1948—a few months after their arrival—with a request not untypical of their early clients. He wanted a low-cost, custom-made modern house, and, in this instance, he wanted to build much of it himself. The Ingrahams complied. They designed a modest, one-story, flat-roofed house for Fundingsland. After that, the work snowballed.[82]

Having worked in Chicago for several years and then in Aspen, the Ingrahams were experienced architects before they set up their own shop in Colorado Springs, but now they had to accommodate marriage, family, and a business in which they were the sole partners. Michael, their first child, was born in 1948 and Catherine followed in 1950. By 1960 they would have two more daughters, Christine and Anna. Elizabeth did most of the parenting and domestic work, in addition to writing contracts, specifications, and business correspondence. In the early 1950s she also kept all the books and did the engineering. Blessed with extraordinary energy, she was nonetheless resentful of the load she carried.

Both Gordon and Elizabeth designed, but on a particular project one or the other took the lead. "From the start we both believed that design was created in one person's head and remained there," Elizabeth said.[83] "A team could bring the building in, doing all the other work together, but the design concept and scheme for a given building belonged to one person only. Gordon and I recognized that one person would do the design and the other would offer support. On the working drawings, we just *did* them. We got the work done and it was not competitive. Our clients typically didn't know which was the designer, and that's the way we wanted it. Eventually, the issue of design, and who did it, created problems but we were okay with it at first."[84]

When a job started both Ingrahams met with the client and developed the program. On residential projects they explored basic values and daily routines. Where would the clients eat breakfast? How did they like to entertain? Where would the children play—and study? What were the clients' interests? They paid close attention and were regarded as exceptional listeners. They also paid attention to the site, seeking marriage of building and terrain that was visually appealing and environmentally prudent. After the introductory "getting to know you" sessions, the Ingrahams went home—back to the studio—to discuss the program. Who would take the lead? "It was pretty even," Elizabeth remembered.[85]

Fig. 15.
Elizabeth and Gordon Ingraham with clients Robert and Mildred Beadles, Colorado Springs, Colorado, 1951. The Ingrahams attracted young families who were looking for something different than the typical postwar tract house. The architects visited their construction sites every day and gained a reputation for close attention to client needs.

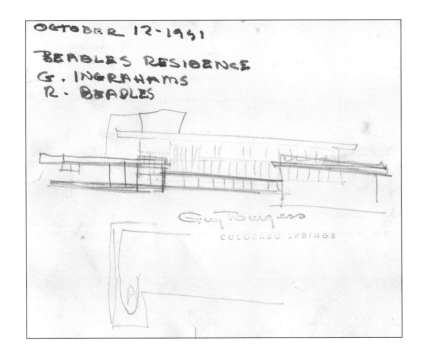

Fig. 16.
Reverse side of Guy Burgess's photograph of the Ingrahams and Beadleses, showing a sketch, 1951.

Oddly enough, it was Gordon who maintained a passion for Frank Lloyd Wright, especially his Usonian house concept.[86] It was Gordon who had studied at Taliesin—not Elizabeth—and despite the almost overwhelming architectural legacy of her family, Elizabeth was more inclined to follow the example of Mies van der Rohe and others who designed in the International Style. The Ingrahams shared a commitment to modern architecture but often disagreed on where to go with it. But in the early years, when they were young, when anything seemed possible, they stuck together to create a body of work fashioned after Wright's famed "natural house."

Although Wright's principles ruled in Ingraham design, each of their houses was designed for particular clients on a particular site. Fifty years later, daughter Catherine considered the houses as an integrated, relational body of work. "Their work was all of a piece—each one different but all related."[87] She spoke of the poured concrete floors with heating systems underneath. "The floors were great, cool in summer and warm in winter."[88] Many of the early houses had narrow floor-to-ceiling windows that were also doors. Redwood siding inside and out was the signature material, bringing texture and line to the interior—as opposed to white plaster walls—but making the rooms dark. Catherine liked the redwood and found its effect to be much like the concrete floors—shady and cool in summer and warm in winter. "There is a sense of enclosure that is quite profound."[89] She also noted the singularity of each home's entry, "Often, one enters in secret, protected ways."[90]

Michael and Catherine Ingraham were infants when the first houses went up, but they lived in and among them for their entire childhood and have strong allegiances and reactions to their parents' work, as do the later children, Christine and Anna. "We were very proprietary," Catherine said.[91] "In the neighborhood [on the Mesa] we considered houses by other designers to be inferior by definition. They were clunkier. We were aware of all the other houses, and we were in many of them often. We compared. We had opinons. We were like little mini-architectural critics."[92] Catherine pointed to the innovations and hallmarks of her parents' designs: courtyards with multiple access, changing floor and ceiling levels, overhanging eaves to regulate light, partial walls on the interior to control circulation and sight lines.

Anna, the youngest, remembered the Beadleses' house: "That long entryway with the corridor that goes all the way back. I liked the entryways of their houses. They kind of lure you in. You don't just walk in the door. Sometimes there was a path or walkway outside the house that prepared you for entering. In the [Wood] Peterson house, the entryway suddenly takes you downstairs into a spacious living room. I thought the houses on the Mesa were wonderful."[93] Her older sister, Christine, appreciated the heated floors but also the overall pattern of each house, where the flow of space and its expression on the exterior dominated any single feature. "They were not interested in features per se, such as bathrooms and kitchens, but saw them as part of the whole. Spatial and lighting concerns were important to Liz, and are still."[94]

Compared to the more ambitious American houses of the late twentieth century, the Ingraham residences were modest in cost and economical in design. Some of that came from the circumstances of the client, but much of the scale resulted from basic Ingraham values, which were shared by the client and were part of the national ethos of the time. About the early fifties houses, Christine Ingraham commented: "There was nothing lavish then. It was all about equality."[95] Bedrooms were always small, bathrooms lean, and kitchens efficient in the manner of a laboratory. Catherine credits her mother

Fig. 17.
1228 Terrace
Road, Colorado
Springs,
Colorado, 1955.
Architects,
Ingraham and
Ingraham. The
house, part of
the Mesa
Terrace
development,
became the
Ingraham
family home.

with mastering the spatial economy of their early homes—the three-dimensional relationships, the intellectual relationships, the total system of each building. "She imagined the whole project and managed it. She was aware of how it worked and how everyone had to work together to accomplish it."[96] She describes Gordon as more painterly, sensitive to beauty. "He worked to acquire a sense of grace and to express that in his house designs."[97]

Eschewing furniture, the Ingrahams used built-ins throughout their houses, much as Frank Lloyd Wright did. Cabinets, chests of drawers, closets, shelves, pull-down tables, banquettes—all of these attached features made rooms look integrated and spare. "They didn't use furniture," Christine recalled.[98] "For years after I left home I didn't have any furniture, and my home today is very spare, very modern."[99] The children, led by their parents, grew up conscious of design everywhere and in all circumstances. "How books were arranged, a table, a room. It was all about design. Even a little dorm room—how would you arrange it? You had to be judging all the time."[100]

Michael Ingraham, still a young child when the family moved to a home and studio on Mesa Terrace, recalls the enormous energy and hard work of his parents in the studio.

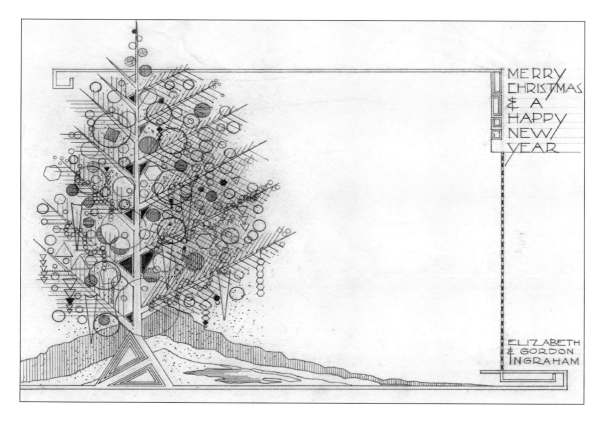

MERRY
CHRISTMAS
& A
HAPPY
NEW
YEAR

ELIZABETH
& GORDON
INGRAHAM

Fig. 18. Christmas card, ca. 1955. The Ingrahams celebrated holidays with friends and family, designing cards and making individual gifts to fit each occasion.

"They worked all the time. Twelve-hour days and into the nights. There was never any money, ever."[101] But he remembers the early days as totally positive. "Gordon and Elizabeth were always home, designing."[102] He has a mental image of them working: Gordon leaning against the drafting table, Elizabeth perched on a stool. "They went out to the site a lot and paid attention to construction. They were very active with workmen. They would rip stuff out and were quick to adapt, doing it on the spot to keep the project moving along. They would tweak the thing right there."[103] As a child, Michael prowled around the neighborhood, often at night, inspecting the construction sites, learning how each house was put together.

The Ingraham children grew up with a degree of freedom that would give nightmares to parents of later generations. They played in the drafting room while their parents worked. They explored the neighborhood. Christine remembers walking barefoot in the summer to downtown, two miles away, whenever she pleased. Their bedrooms had direct access to the outdoors and they were allowed to play on the roof. Meals were minimalist, haphazard affairs. "We ate macaroni and cheese out of a box," Christine recalled.[104] Anna, the youngest, is more forceful: "Liz and Dad were terrible cooks. They did not cook. My husband is a good cook and he is appalled at the way I do it, which is probably what I learned at home."[105] But life was not totally laissez-faire. All the children were good students and later went to excellent colleges. They are an exceptionally articulate family—argumentative and opinionated—committed to a vigorous give-and-take.

Although the Ingraham children fended for themselves in many respects, their parents imposed a great deal of structure, some of it celebratory, some of it disciplinary. They staged festive events at Christmas and Easter, exchanging homemade presents within the family and with friends. Gordon in his memoirs speaks with pride of their holiday parties and the happy expectation that friends developed about the gatherings over the years. Catherine recalls them: "Christmas was a huge holiday. Easter, too. And the Fourth of July. A big deal. And these holidays always connected with the house. The egg hunt. The Christmas tree. These were aesthetic influences and all the kids loved these occasions."[106]

Creating and manipulating an environment, making it work day in and day out—these goals were integral to the design. Part of the idea of a well-planned, economical, customized design was to guarantee that both look and function remained central to the house as a family used it. In her own house, with her own family, Elizabeth took that principle one step further. Of necessity, with a family of six in a small house, some order was required. But beyond necessity, Elizabeth strived for an environment that was deliberately conceived and then meticulously maintained. It was not about cleanliness, per se, but about stewarding one's space, making the most of it, being mindful of both its limitations and possibilities. Catherine remembers the Saturday chores as a way of imposing order on their environment. Elizabeth required the children to do things in a certain way and they became experts. "Michael was very good at doing the floors—cleaning, waxing, buffing—and he did them all. I was the bathroom expert. I would clean and order everything and then bring in a spray of leaves or flowers from outdoors. I was also very good at closets. The idea is to take care of what you have and it's about an underlying order. The space and the living are connected, part of a theory of life. Of course, as kids, we would have rather done something else on Saturday mornings."[107] Michael describes the Saturday chores as being "driven like slaves."[108] The children would polish every object, clean every closet. "We are all of us today terrific cleaners."[109]

Because they maintained the house, the children knew it intimately. They understood the materials, the space, the storage, every detail of its design. In a sense, they kept it alive. They were family, but they were also clients and caretakers. For them and for families in the Ingraham houses that surrounded them, the structures were more than form and function. In Japanese fashion, the houses prescribed an aesthetic and mandated the routines of living. It was an architecture of intimacy, where family lived away from the public eye, enveloped in everyday rituals. But it was also an architecture of hospitality, where occupants entertained neighbors and friends in commemoration of life's passages.

Chapter Four

Four Ingraham Houses From the Early Nineteen Fifties

The Tilley House

The Beadles House

The Wood-Peterson House

The First Vradenburg House

The Tilley House

When the Ingrahams moved to Colorado Springs they remodeled a carriage house near Colorado College on Peacock Alley that served as both home and studio. Their neighbors included Martha and Lewis Tilley—both young artists—and other unconventional free spirits who formed a little bohemia in this very conservative city. The Tilleys soon became clients of the Ingrahams and together they created a highly original, hand-built house on one of the most dramatic sites in the city. The Ingrahams were just getting started in their practice, which they operated out of the newly renovated carriage house. The Tilley house was an early design statement of the Ingrahams and remains one of their most interesting buildings.

Martha and Lew Tilley were both at the Colorado Springs Fine Arts Center School studying painting and other media. Later, Lew joined the faculty. They lived nearby in a "dismal furnished room."[110] As they wheeled their infant daughter on daily strolls through the neighborhood, they would stop to admire an unusual piece of land below the art center's parking lot. The property faced Monument Valley Park and backed up to a twenty-five-foot-high stone wall supported by buttresses. The Tilleys abandoned their lugubrious rented room, bought the vacant lot, and moved temporarily to Peacock Alley, where they met the Ingrahams and soon became clients.

How did they begin the designer/client dialogue? Martha Tilley recalled: "We were friends. We had conversations. They asked questions. We described what we liked and how we wanted to live. They gave us what we wanted."[111] The Tilleys were intriguing clients, totally unconventional and willing to take risks, but the financial constraints were daunting. When a contractor's bid estimate came in at $27,000, they decided to do the project themselves, with an initial $5,000 loan. After that it was pay-as-you-go. Acting as their own contractor, they hired workmen and building specialists when they had to and did much of the work themselves.

After preparing the irregular terrain by leveling and in-filling, Lew Tilley laid the foundations, and John Wright, Elizabeth Ingraham's brother, built a retaining wall to the west of the house site. Another subcontractor laid out the heating system in the concrete floor. Hollow cement blocks placed in the floor circulate heat from a furnace located in the fireplace core at the center of the house.

The walls, both inside and out, and the fireplace core are made of hollow clay tile manufactured in Pueblo, Colorado. The twelve-inch-by-twelve-inch tiles were incised and the resulting ribbed blocks were fired to a muted rosy-gold color, creating a rich and varied texture throughout. The workman alternated laying the tile horizontally and vertically, giving further variety to the surface. Martha Tilley remembers the mason as at least seventy-five years old "and drunk a good deal of the time."[112]

The usual workmen and contractors shied away from the project—too modern, too many unknowns, and therefore too many opportunities for substandard work and lawsuits. Martha recalls another mason finishing the concrete floor, which, once begun, had to be done all of a piece. Working on his hands and knees, he spat tobacco juice on the concrete to keep it moist as he leveled and finished each section. The floor and its polished finish have survived intact after fifty years of family use.

A wooden door, edged with colored glass, opens into the living area just opposite the fireplace. Originally, the 1,450-square-foot house flowed around the large, double-fireplace core, completely open except for the bathroom. Banks of windows, installed to open as doors, line the east and south walls. Unlike many other Ingraham houses, this one has no single, secret or hidden entrance snaking into the house; instead a dozen "doors" line up on two sides of the house to lead one inside on fair-weather days. The house has a sense of openness and easy access, but at the same time its isolated siting gives an air of privacy and seclusion. Overhanging eaves and cloth awnings offer shade in summer.

After the Tilleys moved into the house late in 1949—now with two infants—Martha gradually completed the interior work. She was untrained for carpentry but followed the design drawings in a "literal, laborious way."[113] To save money, she went to a used-lumber yard to rummage through tailings for cheap quarter-sawn redwood boards for the window sashes and ceiling. After seven years she declared the house finished and considered subsequent improvements to be remodeling. The Ingrahams supervised the project, and occasionally the Tilleys hired Gordon to work for them. "They were as poor as we were," Martha said.[114]

The Tilleys and Ingrahams shared an appreciation for hospitality. The house, with its open plan, decks, and large courtyard, accommodated many visitors. Their crowd was wired to the synergism of energetic, aspiring artists and young professionals. "We had lots of parties. I would make a big pot of chicken and rice and people brought their own bottle. Everybody drank hard liquor in those days. Life was a party. Life was painting, cooking, eating, drinking, having fun. People thought nothing of driving when they were drunk. It was a different era."[115]

Tilley family members have occupied the house for more than fifty years. Martha, now the single resident, finds it as comfortable and compatible as when they first lived in it.

Fig. 19.
Tilley house, Colorado
Springs, Colorado,
1949. Architects,
Ingraham and
Ingraham. Terraces,
stone walls, and decks
surround the house,
creating a sense of
shelter in a highly
urbanized area of
the city.

Fig. 20.
Tilley house. Deck
floorboards and a
railing combine with
wide, overhanging
eaves and strip windows
to create a strong
horizontal line. Even the
alternating pattern of
the clay tiles fails to halt
the horizontal sweep.

Fig. 21.
Tilley house. Artist Vincent O'Brien's stained-glass panels elaborate the simple front door. Ducts under the concrete floor provide radiant heat.

Fig. 22.
Tilley house. Originally the house had an open plan. A wall to the right of the fireplace now separates a bedroom from the main area. A double fireplace opposite the entry dominates the living room. Artist Edgar Britton created the sculptures on the small table. Lew Tilley painted the center picture, which is flanked by Boardman Robinson oil paintings.

Fig. 23.
Tilley house.
Canvas strips,
draped under
the open
eave, temper
the sun's glare
in the entry
court.

Fig. 24.
Tilley house
site plan. A
unique
wedge-
shaped site
with high
stone walls on
two sides
dictates the
house
footprint.

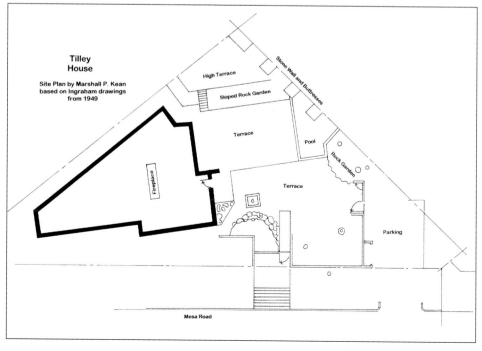

The Beadles House

By 1951, the Tilleys were settled into their walled-in, one-room house, and the Ingrahams had worked through the construction phase of houses for Myron Wood and Edgar Britton, just a mile away on the Mesa. Edgar and Margaret Britton fit into the artist/client model that seemed such a comfortable fit with the Ingrahams. Edgar was a sculptor and Margaret a ceramicist. Myron Wood, a photographer, fit the mold as well. He and the Brittons were part of the admittedly wild, exuberant, hard-drinking, hard-working creative crowd in which the Ingrahams moved. Young professionals moving into Colorado Springs linked up with the lively group and some of them, too, became Ingraham clients.

Robert and Mildred Beadles (he was a urologist and she a schoolteacher) looked at the Tilley, Britton, and Wood homes and were drawn to them immediately. They had been reading books on modern architecture and were pleased to learn about the Ingrahams, who lived nearby and were part of their social circle. Although the Beadleses realized from the start that they were more conservative than the Ingrahams and their other clients, they were determined to have a modern house. They never regretted their choice.

The Ingrahams paid close attention to their clients' wishes. "They were good listeners," Robert Beadles said about the exploratory sessions together that resulted in a three-bedroom, flat-roofed home very much in the Ingraham mold.[116] Except for adding three slot windows in the entry hall, the Beadleses asked for no changes to the initial drawings, which most architects would consider a remarkably restrained client response.

The architects involved themselves in the construction, with Elizabeth acting as contractor as well as supervising architect. The artist Bishop Nash, a veteran of both the Wood and Tilley construction, was part of the team, along with Dewey Dearing, a young architect eager to learn more about the building business. Dearing later married the daughter of A. Jan Ruhtenberg, another modernist designer who had settled in Colorado Springs. Finding experienced workmen sympathetic to the design remained a challenge. The same inebriated mason who had installed the clay tiles on the Tilley house came to work for the Beadleses and appeared to do a creditable job.

Through his church choral group, Robert Beadles recruited a seasoned carpenter named Ed Bodenstein to anchor the construction crew. A taciturn perfectionist, Bodenstein brought rigor to the project and deftly maneuvered the customized, hand-crafted features of the house. He was particularly helpful in creating the built-in cabinetry that was so essential to the home's efficiency. And he kept a close watch on other workmen.[117]

The Beadles home is rich in detail—like other Ingraham houses and Wright's Usonians as well—but manages to retain an austere, modern look. This seeming contradiction stems from the simultaneous use of streamlined features and richly articulated materials.

The arrangement of space is open and straightforward, if somewhat unpredictable. Exterior window and door surrounds are unadorned. The cantilevered overhanging eaves are underlined with plain boards. Inside, the living room's floor-to-ceiling brick fireplace has neither mantel nor any decorative trim. The muted colors and rectilinear characteristics of the painted mural below the living room reinforce the overall contemporary motif. Painted by Eric Bransby, the mural reflects the influence of Josef Albers, with whom Bransby had been studying at Yale. "Yes, there's a bit of Albers in that," Bransby recalled.[118]

It is the profusion of line, much of it created by the materials themselves, that make the early Ingraham houses so complex and nuanced. As is often the case, the entry tells the story. One could argue that the entry extends from the street all the way to the very back wall of the house. Beginning near the curb, the front sidewalk unites with an interior corridor that forms a continuous line from front to back. A door midway opens and closes, but it is merely a transitional interruption along a passageway that extends from the street in front halfway back to the property line. Visitors traverse the entry walk, climb eight stairs, continue along a passageway to the front door and then, upon entering, continue at least visually along a corridor that ends with the south exterior wall of a sitting room.

Fig. 25. Beadles house, Colorado Springs, Colorado, 1951. Architects, Ingraham and Ingraham. A brick patio on the west side of the house serves as an outdoor room. Tent-like fabric strips under the eaves stretch on wire across the patio to create afternoon shade. Visual access through the mitred window adds to the indoor-outdoor flow.

Fig. 26.
Beadles house. An unusual entry—part open, part enclosed—takes the visitor from the front walk, under the carport roof, up eight concrete stairs, and along a narrow porch to the front door. Inside, the narrow walkway resumes as an interior corridor moving to the very end of the house.

Fig. 27.
Beadles house. The north-south axis, reinforced by brick coursing and redwood panels, pulls the eye all the way to the south wall of the house, past the dining room on the right and living room on the left. Ceramic floor tiles replace earlier cork coverings.

Fig. 28.
Beadles house.
Large crossbeams
intersect with
window columns
opposite the raised
living room. The
effect is one of
openness and light
combined with
structural solidity.

Fig. 29.
Beadles house.
Three posts mark
entry to a
bedroom and
bath area and act
as a counterpoint
to the strong
horizontal lines of
the house. The
mural at lower right
is the work of Eric
Bransby, who
credits the
influence of artist
Josef Albers, with
whom Bransby
studied at Yale
University.

The long journey getting in is reinforced by lines—of the sidewalk itself, of the redwood siding planks, of the roof overhang that acts as a partial shelter over the narrow front porch. The sensation is one of leaving the outside world to enter a tunnel that ends with the front door. Once inside, the redwood planks continue, both along the walls and on the ceiling. They pull the eye forward to the end of the house and momentarily exclude other spaces. Then, moving to the core of the house, one finds a small dining area connecting with the kitchen, and, in the opposite direction, a raised living room accessed by a wide, shallow staircase. Here, in the center, the dynamics change. The seemingly dominant horizontal line that forms a north-south axis now gives way to strong verticals formed by the floor-to-ceiling windows of the west wall. Redwood ceiling planks overhead are intersected by powerful wooden beams that link up with the window framing. Thus, as the center core of the house is revealed and the eye goes from left to right, the linear entry journey is interrupted by opposing lines. No diagonals exist in this house, only straight lines and right angles. And while the horizontal rules, vigorous vertical elements both define and break up spaces.

The profusion of line inside and out is carried by the redwood siding, but additional pattern emerges in the masonry of walls, floors, and fireplace. Square clay tiles cover the dining and kitchen floors. The living room floor, now carpeted, was originally faced with cork tiles, widely used in the 1950s. Brick walls and the brick fireplace add further texture, color, and line to the interior surfaces, tending to break up large areas into very small modules that are linked together in the whole. The effect is of a rich and varied surface pattern that counteracts the spare modern lines of the overall design.

The Beadles house offers generous access to the outdoors. A large patio on the east and south services both the dining and living rooms and is visually accessible from these public areas. A brick wall west of the house frames the patio space, offering intimacy and privacy.

The Beadleses raised three children in their new home—two daughters and a son. At first, the large living room served as a family area where the children studied and played and where Mildred Beadles sewed. Banquettes for seating lined the walls. Cork and ceramic tile floors were in keeping with a low-maintenance credo. The Beadleses considered the house ideal for family life. "The children loved the house," she said, "and we feel they are artistic and innovative."[119] When the couple entertained, the house and patio easily accommodated fifty people. Guests could go in and out easily, circling around from patio to living room to dining room.

Their friends liked the house "for the most part," Robert Beadles said.[120] "We had a doctor friend in Carroll, Iowa, who lived in a Cape Cod cottage. He and his wife saw our house and decided they wanted one just like it."[121] The Ingrahams designed the Iowa house a year later. "Their neighbors were fascinated. These houses, with their poured concrete floors and fireplaces and partial brick walls, look very different from the standard frame house when they're going up. One of the things that other people appreciate—as we do—is the graceful flow of the house. We have privacy but you can see from one room to the next and into the outdoors. It's restful for the eye. A surgeon's life is stressful. On those days that I came home for lunch, the house was so peaceful, so serene. I would lie down in this living area and feel relaxed and renewed."[122]

From the start the Beadleses liked the mitred-corner glass in the sitting room. The view to the patio is unobstructed and the pattern of the redwood ceiling boards continues

Fig. 30.
Beadles house.
A brick pier
anchors the
house core
where living
room, dining
room, and patio
intersect. The
glass abuts the
brick directly, an
example of the
Ingrahams's
exacting
craftsmanship.
The Eric Bransby
mural,
interrupted by
stairs to the
living room,
resumes for the
length of the
hallway.

Fig. 31.
Beadles
house, plan.

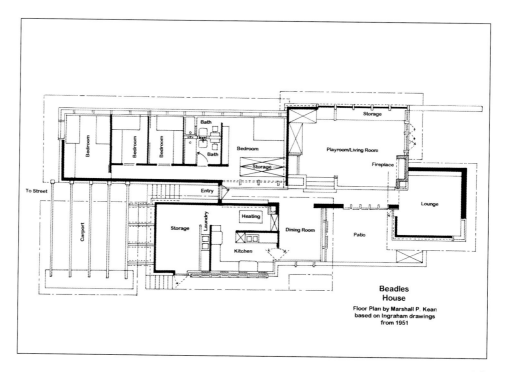

Beadles
House

Floor Plan by Marshall P. Kean
based on Ingraham drawings
from 1951

Fig. 32. Beadles house. A tiny shoji screen on the serving counter closes the kitchen off from the dining room. When open, the screen reveals a mosaic mural that runs the counter's length. Built-in cupboards and drawers offer efficient storage and add a rich wood patina to the dining room scheme.

above the window glass to form the underside of the roof overhang. The indoors going out and vice versa pleased the clients. They remained equally fond of the kitchen, with its efficient appointments and pleasant view toward the scenic west.

In retrospect, the Beadleses identified a few things they would have done differently. They would change the radiant floor-heating system, which they find hard to control. They would use duct heat instead and make the windows double paned. At the time of construction, heating oil and gas were cheap and no one considered efficiencies. The reality of cold, or perhaps just the perception of cold, drove them to cover the concrete walls of their bedroom and bath with wallpaper. "The Ingrahams didn't want us to do that," Robert Beadles said, "but we insisted."[123]

The Beadleses' satisfaction with the house stemmed from their admiration of the designers as much as it did from the work itself. Mildred Beadles described the Ingrahams as visionaries with strong values but willing to respect their clients' tastes and ideals. "They were intolerant of selfishness and imperfection. They were concerned about the environment and creative in the use of the land. They were loyal friends and had wonderful kids. They were humble in many respects."[124]

Attentive architects. Happy clients. Houses nearly unchanged after fifty years. An unusual story and one that underscores the intensity of the modernist dream as it played out at mid-century. Only a small fraction of the nation's new homeowners chose modern, but those who did tended to be passionate believers.

The Wood-Peterson House

As you approach the quintessential Ingraham house for the first time, two sensations dominate your consciousness: first, the business of getting in, and then, once in, of looking back out. In the tradition of Frank Lloyd Wright, entries can be hard to find, more like secret passages than the standard, familiar front door. Asymmetrically placed, sometimes hidden, these entries offer only a minor break with the exterior world. You slip in, tentative, unsure. Is this the right house? The right door?

At the Wood-Peterson house, you enter the main door directly into a studio added in 1987, which places you almost immediately on the threshold of the original 1950 main house. On opening the second door, you first glimpse a wooden wall directly opposite, hung with paintings. Stepping inside to a stair landing, you are aware of a hallway up to the left leading away from the stairs to the back of the house. Turning right and standing near the head of the stairway, you then see the full drama of this remarkable house. A small window at eye level frames Pikes Peak, ten miles to the west. Directly below, following the wood stairs, you come to a second landing, this of grey polished concrete that also forms the floor of a large fireplace on the right, covered by a sweeping copper hood reaching to the ceiling.[125]

The stairway has no railing. You are steadied on the right by a mammoth wall of layered rough concrete and native sandstone poured in the manner of Frank Lloyd Wright's home and studio at Taliesin West in Scottsdale, Arizona. Here on the second landing you are in the heart of the living area. The dining room and kitchen extend toward the back of the house, parallel to the long stairway, and in front, the living room walls converge to a wedge, like the prow of a ship.

More desert masonry reminiscent of Taliesin West anchors the bank of south-facing, floor-to-ceiling windows of the living room opening onto a courtyard. Redwood ceiling planks follow the east-west axis of the stairway, angling to follow the wall wedge. Lines are everywhere: vertical lines formed by seams on the sweeping copper fireplace hood and by the floor-to-ceiling window frames, horizontal lines in the layered masonry and redwood ceiling and cabinetry.

A sense of tight control and discipline is manifest in these rigorous lines. But the order is countered by the surprises of the spatial flow and even more by the desert masonry, nowhere more evident than in the exterior wall abutting the fireplace. Standing in the dining area, you see a dozen or more rectangular shapes that form the stairway and, above it, the bricks and hood of the large, open fireplace. It is all very regular, all very structured—all except the masonry wall, which introduces an element of collision

Fig. 33. Wood-Peterson house, Colorado Springs, Colorado, 1950. Architects, Ingraham and Ingraham. Entry stair, as viewed from the living room. Flat fieldstones, set in poured concrete, trigger the room's dynamics. The long sweep of overhead paneling meets crosscurrent lines of stairs and built-in cabinets and shelves. Copper sheathing over the fireplace rises high above the stair landing and hearth.

and danger. The huge sandstones embedded in the concrete appear to hurtle down the stairs. They are not "solid as a rock" but instead appear suspended in air, if not actually falling. This dramatic intersection of lines, the slightly dangerous evocation of the masonry, and the flow of space—as though rushing from the upper hall, down the stairs, and towards the ship-like prow—all create an exhilarating, slightly unsettling sense of vertigo.

The exhilaration experienced by a first-time visitor to the house translates to a compelling daily ritual for the residents. Each describes the staircase as the most satisfying, salient feature of the house, especially appreciated in the first minutes of the day when, from the first landing just off the master bedroom, one sees the distant mountain and then the house interior revealed below. After forty years, the element of surprise is gone but the vivid sense of daring remains.

Fig. 34. Wood-Peterson house. The fieldstones appear to hurtle down the stairs.

Fig. 35. Wood-Peterson house. A cabinet and shelves screen the kitchen without hindering visual access from the dining room.

Fig. 36.
Wood-Peterson house. A pier of layered concrete and fieldstone penetrates the living area. The redwood paneling overhead assumes a complex pattern often used by the Ingrahams.

E. R. (Pete) and Judith Peterson were predisposed to buy an Ingraham house. A professor of French and a Dada scholar, he was attracted to modernist architecture early on. "Actually, I first got interested in Tristan Tzara and Dada through a building, through a house that the Viennese architect Adolf Loos did for Tzara in Paris, in Montmartre. Loos designed a house in Paris for Josephine Baker, too, but it was never built. Tzara was also a friend of Le Corbusier. I took a walking tour in Paris in 1949 and saw the house. I didn't come back to Tzara for a few years, but I remembered that really interesting house and it stuck in my mind."[126]

A dozen years later the Wood house, just off Mesa Road in Colorado Springs, struck the Petersons as "a really interesting house" as well. A cluster of twelve Ingraham houses formed a loosely knit development called Mesa Terrace. A few houses by architect Walt Weber, a contemporary of the Ingrahams, stood nearby on the narrow gravel roads that curved through the neighborhood. Many of the homes and the residents in them proved to be compatible. The Ingrahams lived and worked just down the hill.

They and the Petersons became friends immediately. Children roamed freely in these accepting, safe environs. "Everyone was good to them," Pete Peterson recalls. "It's been a pleasure from beginning to end—forty years—and not many changes in the neighborhood."[127]

Judith Peterson describes their house purchase as intuitive and subjective. They knew something of Frank Lloyd Wright's work and felt comfortable with the Ingraham house from the start. She saw it as relatively carefree in its maintenance and therefore an

Fig. 37. Wood-Peterson house. Desert masonry piers flank the master bedroom. The dining and living room area fronts on the patio, which is shaded by a mature apple tree.

appealing family home. After the Petersons moved in, John Wright, Elizabeth's brother and an accomplished craftsman, built banquette seats along the north wall of the living room and a desk in the master bedroom. Although the Petersons made many changes over the years, they respected their home's original lines and materials.

Myron Wood, the first owner, came back to the house from time to time to take photographs. He and Bishop Nash, an artist, had worked alongside Gordon Ingraham on portions of the original construction, struggling together on the Taliesin-style desert masonry, keeping the sandstones in place as concrete layers were poured to form exterior walls. They had covered the stones with cheesecloth and newspaper, then poured the concrete, and—after the walls had set—scraped the stones clean.

In the late 1970s, the Petersons brought Gordon back to design an addition of two bedrooms connected to the main house by a glassed-in bridge. This became the children's wing. A few years later they added a playroom on the site of the carport, adjacent to the new bridge. They remember Gordon as a thoughtful designer, sensitive to costs and to making the new area fit the rest of the house. He was meticulous in his attention to details.

A few years later, anticipating that Judith's mother would live with them, the Petersons hired Elizabeth Ingraham to draw up a new wing where the carport stood. "Elizabeth was sensitive to mother's needs, including privacy. She urged us to do a sitting room as well as a bedroom and bath so she could have guests and lead her own life. But mother died a month before it was finished."[128] The sitting room is now a studio for Judith and the bedroom a library for the professor.

Like other Ingraham houses of this era, the floors are polished poured concrete, covered in part with area rugs. The bedroom/bath area on the upper level is carpeted to make the rooms warmer and the floors more comfortable underfoot. Single-pane windows and walls with little insulation were the standard in 1950 when gas prices were low, but the house would be built differently today, with a greater concern for economy and comfort. The house siting, however, facing south with deep overhangs, offers sun in the winter and shade in summer.

Built into a hillside, the house backs into a slope that flattens to form a courtyard paved with red sandstone. Mindful of Colorado's semiarid climate, the Ingrahams eschewed grass and kept plantings simple—native shrubs, coniferous trees, and the ubiquitous juniper bushes, the hallmarks of 1950s landscapes.

From the courtyard the house rises two stories, the glassed-in living and dining rooms receding beneath the flat overhangs of the extended roof. Masonry piers and an overhanging redwood-sided upper floor dominate the south façade. The house from this vantage suggests the defensive style of indigenous Southwest architecture. Even the tin-clad roof beams that thrust into the edge of the courtyard are reminiscent of Spanish canales, the rain spouts common to early New Mexico buildings.

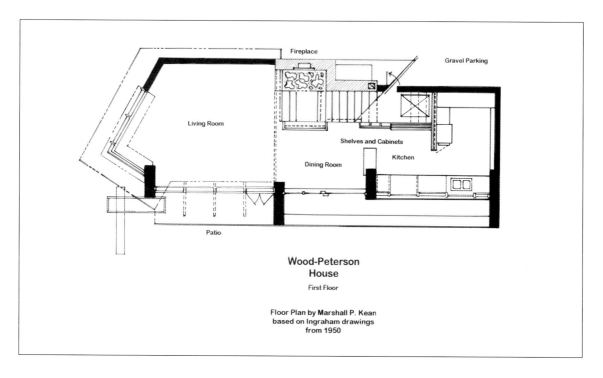

Figs. 38 and 39. Wood-Peterson house. First-floor plan (above), second-floor plan (below).

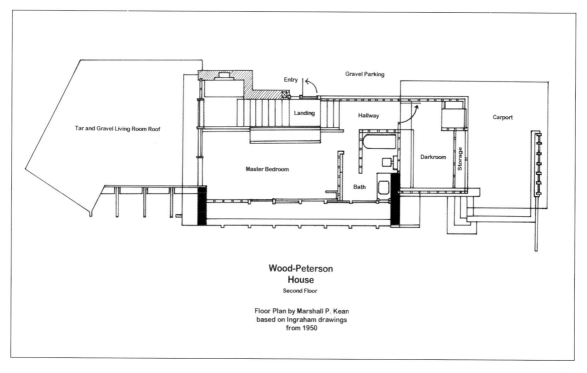

The First Vradenburg House

A hundred yards south of the Wood-Peterson house, the first Vradenburg house occupies identical terrain and a similar site. Built in 1950 and designed originally for a family that abandoned the project because of the breadwinner's ill health, the house was adapted to meet the needs of clients George and Bee Vradenburg. As volunteer manager of the Colorado Springs Symphony, Bee wanted a house suitable for entertaining. Later, the Vradenburgs commissioned a second, larger house on the Mesa, again designed by the Ingrahams. The first Vradenburg house incorporates most of the features and materials that were quickly becoming the Ingrahams's signature: flat roof, carport, banks of windows to the south and west, a copious use of redwood inside and out, a strong regard for the outdoors, open plan, compact kitchen, and a curious and complicated entrance.[129]

You approach the house from the south, down a short driveway that leads to a double carport. From here you head west, along a stone-paved portico supported by five wood columns. At the end of the porch, there are two choices: to enter a gated deck and head towards a wooden door that appears to access the upper level, or, proceeding past the slanted supports of the deck, to descend seven stone stairs to a courtyard. The entry lies before you on the south façade: a glass box with mitred corners, very much in the Wrightian manner, that surrounds a modest wooden door. Inside, a four-foot wall allows you visual access to the living and dining area but guides you to the right where stone stairs, much like those on the deck, take you to the upper floor.

If you turn around upon entering to look back outdoors, you see a collision of competing lines: the horizontal wood dividers of the glass entry windows, the perpendicular cross-hatching of redwood planks under the eaves, cinder blocks that form the exterior walls, the sloping, out-thrust walls of the deck, columns that hold up the portico, and the stone pavement of the patio floor. This entry, although small in scale and flush with the wall, is rich in forms and line. As the viewer moves, the lines move in a robust and dynamic fashion. Although designing with a grammar often described as spare and without ornament, the architects managed a complex, evolving artistry that seems to set the building in motion.

Although the bedrooms are predictably small, the master bath offers an expansive use of space and materials. Redwood planks create a large storage area between toilet and bath, and enclose a vertical translucent glass light near the tub. The floor tiles and sinks are new, but the redwood cabinetry keeps the room within the spirit of the original house.

Fig. 40.
First Vradenburg
house, Colorado
Springs, Colorado,
1951. Architects,
Ingraham and
Ingraham. Wood
posts brace a
huge overhang
that shelters both
entry and carport.
Access to the
house is from
either the wooden
deck or the stone-
paved patio.

Fig. 41.
First Vradenburg
house. Crossbars
and a mitred
corner create a
spare, modernist
entry. Through the
glass one sees the
lines of overhead
eaves and the
outward-thrusting
deck wall.

Fig. 42.
First Vradenburg
house. A patina of
redwood and
earth-tone tiles
give the bathroom
a warm, rich glow.
Handcrafted
cabinets became
a hallmark of
Ingraham design,
influenced by
Frank Lloyd Wright's
Usonian houses.

Fig. 43.
First Vradenburg
house. The kitchen
lies behind the
wooden door. A
plastered, cement
block partition
defines the dining
space, separating
it from the living
area. The tile floor
is new.

Fig. 44.
First Vradenburg house. The extended flat roof shades an enclosed portico that looks out over the Mesa towards the mountains. Nine wood columns add formality to the façade.

Clerestory windows, a feature common to both Ingraham and Wright houses, light the upstairs hallway. A long, horizontal fiberglass lamp augments the natural light in this area. An iron railing opens the hall to the living room below. The open plan of this split-level house offers a rich array of visual access.

The living and dining rooms look out towards the west. Nearly the entire wall, supported by nine wood posts, consists of floor-to-ceiling glass. A deep overhang shades both the patio and the interior but allows the afternoon sun to come in during winter.

A thick door lined with horizontal redwood planks closes off the kitchen from the public rooms of the house. Again, clerestory windows to the west bring in light. Somehow, the original wooden cabinets in the kitchen and metal cabinets in the pantry have survived several owners and remain in place. The room is larger than many Ingraham kitchens and has space for a small table and chairs.

The current owners of the house, attorney Kent Borges and physicist Stephanie DiCenzo, toyed with the idea of remodeling the kitchen and then desisted. DiCenzo argues that there is sometimes a fine line between "shabby" and "venerable."[130] They decided after a few months that their never-remodeled, fifty-year-old kitchen was venerable and, over time, they grew more and more attached to it. Emerald green laminate covers the counters, sliding glass panels serve as doors to the original wooden cabinets, metal storage cabinets are in nearly perfect condition in the open pantry.

Purchase of the Vradenburg house was something of a fluke for Borges and DiCenzo. Accustomed to traditional homes in the East, they had supposed they would buy in the Old North End, a neighborhood of turn-of-the-century frame houses north of Colorado College and considered part of the city core. Then DiCenzo saw a classified ad in the local newspaper that listed a "Frank Lloyd Wright Usonian House on the Mesa."[131] It was not, of course, a Wright house, but it was close to the Usonian model he developed, and when they went to look they liked it immediately. They liked the upper-level bedroom suite and the clerestory windows in the kitchen. And they loved the views. With mature evergreens and other shrubs on all sides of the property, window shades are never drawn at night.

The owners find the house comfortable and low maintenance. Unlike most early Ingraham houses, this one did not come with polished concrete floors. Borges and DiCenzo pulled the shag carpet from the living and dining areas to install square ceramic tiles. Perhaps once a year they oil the interior wood with lemon/orange oil. Every few years, the exterior eaves require a coat of stain shellac on the underside. They find the interior redwood dark but like its ambience at night under artificial lights. The open plan and extensive patios create a sense of space and easy access to the outdoors, both visual and physical.

Although Ingraham houses were designed with careful attention to the needs of their original owners, this particular house proves that later buyers can adapt successfully decades later and be content to honor the intent of the architects. The expanses of new floor tile in this house are in keeping with the natural materials credo the Ingrahams followed.

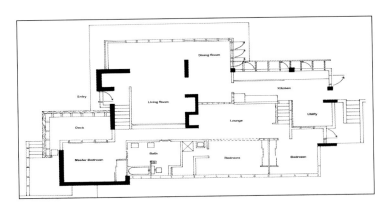

Fig. 45.
First
Vradenburg
house plan.

Afterword

Fig. 46.
Hugh Andersen
house. Cascade,
Colorado, 1952.
Architects,
Ingraham and
Ingraham. Built-in
cabinets, shelves,
and seating were
hallmarks of
Ingraham
residential design.

Fig. 47.
Hugh Andersen house.
Cascade, Colorado,
1952. The Ingrahams
designed fifteen houses
in their first five years of
practice, primarily in
and around Colorado
Springs. Features of the
Andersen house were
very much in keeping
with other Ingraham
designs of that period.

The Work

During their twenty-two-year practice, the Ingrahams designed two guest houses and thirty-five homes, remodeled eight more, added on to twelve, and completed two studio additions. They received four commissions for municipal projects from the city of Pueblo, Colorado, in the 1960s along with several residences, and they operated an office in that city for several years. They designed an elementary school for the main Colorado Springs school district in 1968. Their institutional work included two churches and a rural schoolhouse. In the late 1950s, they completed several houses in the Fargo [ND]-Moorhead [MN] area. Their later work included several site plans and model house plans for a developer, but almost no commercial work. They closed the practice in 1971.

Gordon Ingraham

By the late 1960s, both the Ingraham firm and marriage were troubled and adrift. The partners shut down their Pueblo office in 1966. Gordon went East for six months, working first in Geneva, New York, and then in West Hartford, Connecticut, for architects John Erlich and Warren Ashley. Returning home, Gordon joined in the anti-Vietnam War activity that was consuming the entire Ingraham family. The older children, all teenagers except for Anna, congregated daily with activist friends at the Ingraham house on Terrace Road. Elizabeth started a book on America's younger generation. Gordon counseled students on the draft. Young Anna, born in 1960, has vivid memories of the late 1960s: "Our house was almost a refuge for lots of wayward kids who needed help or who wanted to talk about the confusing things going on in the country and also the world. They wanted a sympathetic place to be and wanted to talk."[132] Michael, a student at Colorado College, worked on the campus antiwar movement and brought his friends back to the house, where they would talk into the night. "The family became very involved in Vietnam. Very."[133]

Gordon and Elizabeth agreed ideologically about the war but participated in different ways. To daughter Christine, their responses reflected basic differences in personality: "Both Gordon and Liz were opposed, but he wasn't as involved in the group activities. Gordon was less socially oriented. He opposed the war but found all the people around all the time to be a distraction. He was a draft counselor. I loved it [the people and commotion]. I'm very social, very gregarious, as Liz is. Gordon wanted more privacy."[134]

The Ingrahams separated in 1971 after several years of strife. Elizabeth remained at 1228 Terrace Road with Christine and Anna. Michael was at the University of Toronto and Catherine at St. John's College in Santa Fe. Gordon lived a peripatetic life during this period, working as a draftsman in a series of architectural offices and moving from place to place. He writes in his memoirs of drinking daily and often excessively. In 1978 he married Mary Bea Gadd, a longtime friend, and they shared a happy relationship until her death in 1984. Gordon stopped drinking about that time and remained sober for the rest of his life.[135] He died in August 1999.

In his later years, Gordon turned to drawing—colored-pencil drawings, mostly of the Southwest. They depict a close-up world of mountain and desert landscapes made mysterious by a complex linearity. Gordon liked to draw. He traveled extensively in the region to photograph and sketch. He sold some of the drawings and shared others with friends and family. Perhaps he was an artist at heart and was more at home drawing landscapes than working at the more functional business of architecture. And perhaps the linear nature of the drawings harkened back to his architectural design, which was so marked by line. The long expanses of redwood siding, the built-ins, the careful attention to detail with every feature, the particularity of brick and tile, the sense of sweep and movement as one enters a room—these expressions are foremost linear.

The Ingraham children saw the artistic side of their father early on. Catherine described his approach to architecture as painterly: "He was extremely interested in and sensitive to beauty and worked to acquire a sense of grace, and to express that in his house designs. He did very good renderings in the Taliesin style, with colored pencils."[136] "He was more of an artist than an architect," Christine concluded.[137] Michael, too, saw the drawings as a substitute for design: "He began to reject the idea of architecture. He took up rendering. His drawings had lots of lines and cross-hatching. He did these drawings for the rest of his life. Some are very good."[138] Anna, the youngest, described him as a "beautiful artist" who loved his work.[139] For Gordon, the drawings were therapeutic as well as artistic. He started them in earnest after Mary Bea died and after he had successfully quit drinking—"My life has been filled with the drawings."[140]

Elizabeth Ingraham

Like Gordon, Elizabeth let go of architecture when they separated in 1971, but for her, design regained a central place later in life. For the next twelve years, Elizabeth concentrated on administering the Wright-Ingraham Institute, founded by her after the break with Gordon. With a mission of environmental sustainability and responsible land use, the institute operated programs in education and public policy, including field research, conferences, and classes.

A gift to the institute of 640 acres near Parker, Colorado, provided a specific terrain for the field work and a gathering place for the entire project. After twelve years and still no funding, the institute was put on hold, supervised by an advisory board, all of them alumni from the 1970s. Although Elizabeth is still the president, she looks forward to a new, young board taking charge. The project remains a passion: "The institute is probably the most meaningful thing I've ever done."[141]

In 1983, Elizabeth went to Africa to visit her daughter Anna, who was serving in the Peace Corps in South Africa. She traveled in Mozambique, Angola, Namibia, Zambia, and Zimbabwe, marveling at both the landscape and the life. From halfway around the world, Elizabeth got her bearings and envisioned a new career in design. During her month in Africa, she identified with the Danish writer Isak Dinesen, author of *Out of Africa*. "I had lost everything," Elizabeth said. "I had no money, no job, no support."[142]

Fig. 48 (left) and Fig. 49 (below) Colored-pencil drawings by Gordon Ingraham. Gordon's drawings explored both the natural and spiritual qualities of the American Southwest.

Fig. 50. Gordon Ingraham, ca. 1990. Gordon did occasional design work in his later years but turned from architecture to concentrate on drawing.

Fig. 51. Vista Grande Community Church, Colorado Springs, Colorado, 1985. Architect, Elizabeth Wright Ingraham. Shortly after opening her firm's office in downtown Colorado Springs, Elizabeth began designing the Vista Grande church and, through it, began to establish a new vernacular using glass and concrete rather than the signature redwood of Ingraham and Ingraham in the 1950s and '60s.

Fig. 52. "La Casa," residence in Pueblo West, Colorado, 1995. Architect, Elizabeth Wright Ingraham. High winds, blowing sand, and blistering sun make the Pueblo site daunting and difficult. Concrete walls and barriers shelter residents from intrusive weather and desert creatures.

Fig. 53. "Solaz," residence of Dawn and Brad Wilde, Manitou Springs, Colorado, 1997. Architect, Elizabeth Wright Ingraham. A concrete wall combines with banks of windows to provide both light and privacy.

Back in Colorado Springs, Elizabeth opened an office on Pikes Peak Avenue in the heart of downtown. Her timing could not have been worse. Colorado had started into a recession that would last through the 1980s. Construction plummeted. Architectural offices and other businesses folded. "I sold a lot of valuable possessions during that time to survive."[143] Two early commissions pulled her through: the Vista Grande Community Church and the Brian Cole house, both in Colorado Springs.

Elizabeth took on other assignments. In the early 1980s, she taught for the University of Colorado Architecture School. Later in the decade she was appointed by then-Governor Richard Lamm to serve on the State Board of Examiners of Architects. Both appointments enlarged her professional circle and both gave her a role in Denver, a city she admires.

Fig. 54.
Elizabeth Wright Ingraham, from
a profile in *Designer/Builder:
A Journal of the Human
Environment*, February 1998.

Chosen from among five firms competing for the Vista Grande church project, Elizabeth felt challenged to create vertical movement within a rectangular space. "It's an economical space," she concluded. "I was trying for a sanctuary above the surrounding subdivisions that related directly to the West and mountains."[144] Working with an open-minded building committee willing to take some risks, Elizabeth focused attention on materials, especially new products on the market. For the exterior walls, she chose insulated concrete—fiberglass set between two layers of poured concrete. This process, now commonplace, was new and untried at the time. Typically, construction innovation sparks warfare between architect and contractor: "There is always a fear factor in the hinterlands—nobody wants to try anything new."[145]

As the sole designer on a project, Elizabeth became very conscious of her creative process, which she describes as an immersion in technical specifics combined with a highly intuitive response to that immersion. "In the process of design, I work to find out the program, the environment, the materials. I design from structure. Form evolves from structure. I immerse myself in the project, but I don't usually work immediately at the drafting table."[146] She discovered an odd associative link that often exists for her between eating and design. As she grappled with the central design idea for the church, she was seated at her dining room table, eating and making sketches. "When it works, there is an

'Aha!' period, and the idea clamps into place. For the church it was a marvelous moment but a tense moment. If I don't get it, don't capture it, then I don't have it. Sometimes it [the 'Aha! moment'] lasts a minute, sometimes a month. Some designers never reach it."[147] The "moment" is clearly one of integration, a kind of epiphany in which the whole is more than the sum of its parts. "When you bring all the factors together then you can move along and get the work done. At a later point you focus on details, which are very important."[148]

The Vista Grande church provided her a major institutional commission, but Elizabeth continued to design houses, as she had done in the early years with Gordon. Her most ambitious project, La Casa, in Pueblo, Colorado, presented fascinating, though rather odd, circumstances for design and construction. Originally, the house comprised about 7,000 square feet [there have been two subsequent additions]. It sits on a 150-foot cliff in desert terrain. The site offered 360-degree views, including the Rocky Mountains to the west. Elizabeth learned from the site engineers that it was too risky to build at the ravine's edge. She elected instead to enclose a 55-foot steel truss through the house that extends above the cliff as a cantilevered skywalk. Elizabeth chose glazed masonry for the exterior, a material capable of withstanding sand storms and blazing sun. Grappling with the site's difficult environment—high winds, extremes in temperature, little moisture—dictated many of the building's design features.

Elizabeth applied her design talents to a more modest project in the late 1990s—a home and studio in Manitou Springs, Colorado, for Dawn and Bradley Wilde.[149] She is a painter; he is a retired Air Force engineer with architectural training. The 3,200-square-foot house salutes certain of Elizabeth's design features from the 1950s—the open plan, window strips, concrete floor—but eschews the signature overleaf eaves in favor of a trim metal cornice that neatly caps the roof edge. She had long ago moved away from

---

"The environment was unbelievably hostile. We killed seventeen rattlesnakes during construction. Winds were as high as 110 miles an hour. We had to make the house a fortress—protect it from the surroundings. No indoor-outdoor Wrightian model here. You did not want that. You had to protect the interior. It was a very difficult job. We had trouble with subcontractors. We had to build a long passageway from the garage to the house so that it was all internal. We replaced glass twice because of hail kicking stones up from the ground. Planted native vegetation there.

The owners had an old three-story house [in Pueblo] full of possessions and they were great consumers. Four moving vans pulled up. I was appalled and never quite saw that coming. They had extremely expensive things and just massive amounts. All this stuff. Everywhere. Up. Down. We have had two additions and probably a third is coming. They now have a big entertainment deck and a special oven to make croissants. I added a guest cottage for the mothers and a bridge to connect it."

Interview with Elizabeth Ingraham, March 13, 2002,
about "La Casa."

---

redwood siding, which, like all wood, does poorly in Colorado's unforgiving bright sunshine. In this instance she chose unfinished concrete block for the exterior and certain interior walls. An exterior *brise-soleil* grid over the entry door extends inside the house and across the living area, creating light and shadow patterns. Vertical and horizontal window strips visually define and outline the façade. The window arrangement ensures maximum light and at the same time reserves interesting wall expanses that can accommodate large paintings. The house was featured in the February 2001 *Architectural Record*.[150]

The Wildes—like many Ingraham clients before them—are passionate about their house, which they have named "Solaz," Spanish for solace. They are captured by the light in its many forms: skylights, expanses of windows, the *brise-soleil*, as well as installed lighting that is part of the architecture. Dawn Wilde savors the early-morning light in the hall and living area. She likes coming home to the lighted house at night. They use blinds in the master bedroom but otherwise avoid window coverings. Brad Wilde admires the drama of windows rising two stories above the southeast patio, a view he sees repeatedly throughout the day as he takes the stairway to and from his office on the first level. This embrace of light puts the house in sharp contrast to the early Ingraham houses of the 1950s, where redwood paneling and deep overhanging eaves darken the interior.

Happily, the Wildes had a handsome collection of Danish modern furniture when they moved in, acquired by Dawn in 1959 during a visit to Denmark. The honey-toned furniture matches the plain wooden cabinet doors in the kitchen and living areas. The overall effect is very much in the Alvar Aalto tradition of spare architecture tempered by warm woods. The Wildes confine clutter to their respective work areas; the public spaces are ordered, in keeping with the basic modern forms. They like the concrete floor and the random patterns created by its pouring.

Solaz more closely resembles the work of Le Corbusier or Mies van der Rohe than it does that of Frank Lloyd Wright, but it is also akin to designs of late-twentieth-century architects such as Houston-based Carlos Jimenez or New York's Architectural Research Office [ARO] team of Adam Yarinsky and Stephen Cassell. These designers turn to metal, glass, and masonry.

Elizabeth's later work shows no influence of the jagged, explosive creations of Daniel Libeskind nor the goofy, biomorphic shapes of Frank Gehry. Both architects gained international prominence in the late twentieth century. Given the vicissitudes of Elizabeth's life and her inherently headstrong, assertive nature, we might expect something more risky, more chaotic, but her design sense dictates economy and discipline. She has opted for a client-shaped practice that produces an architecture of harmony and buildings that reflect the collaborative client role.

Elizabeth keeps her home and professional base in Colorado Springs, despite the city's seeming indifference to her work. She has designed only a handful of new buildings in the past decade, notable projects but few in number. Her children have mixed reactions to Colorado Springs as a proper home for their parents' design work. Michael thinks locating there was a mistake from the start: "The town never supported them. I'm pleased with what they were able to produce, but it's not near what they wanted."[151] Christine only recently put thumbs down on the city: "They accomplished a lot in Colorado Springs, but it might have been a better situation somewhere else with more opportunities for commercial jobs."[152] She and Michael agree that, while their parents were talented designers, they were poor business managers. Anna defends their decision to settle in Colorado: "It was a deliberate decision. They wanted to be in the West, in a small city, away from the big urban centers but around someplace that had promise. It's a very hard profession. Hard to get jobs and get paid."[153] Catherine feels they produced very good work in Colorado Springs: "And I'm not sure things would have been better anywhere else financially. Architecture is tough."[154]

Fundamentally an optimist, Elizabeth senses exciting opportunities ahead for architecture. At the same time, she criticizes the profession for following rather than leading, for attending to the elites rather than the people, and for buckling under to the commercial opportunism of developers, when architects should have been offering alternatives—especially in housing. She sees glass as the material of the future, a transformative material that can spark technological revolution in design. The work of Spanish-born Santiago Calatrava inspires her; she is intrigued with Dutch designer Rem Koolhaas's new Prada store in Manhattan. Both architects have experimented successfully with glass.

The Ingraham children, as they have done all their lives, monitor their mother's professional work. Catherine, Dean of the School of Architecture at Pratt Institute in Brooklyn, connects more with Elizabeth's later work than with the mid-century houses done by both parents, although she admires it all. Michael considers her current work path breaking and credits Elizabeth with being able to grow and change with a changing world, first with the environmental institute and then with her renewed architecture practice. She has always been, in Michael's view, "ahead of her time."[155]

Elizabeth Ingraham exhibits tremendous ambition and a passion for architecture, but in some very crucial ways, she has distracted herself from a focus on design. Gregarious, energetic, and confident, she is a ready recruit for good causes. Early on there was the Colorado Springs Symphony Orchestra to reorganize, then an international exchange program, partisan politics, and a state women's forum. Vietnam antiwar activism claimed much of her life for years, followed by more than a decade at the helm of the Wright-Ingraham Institute. More recently she has headed the American Institute of Architects Colorado Chapter. She lectures and writes. The attraction to power and the drive to shape public policy no doubt get in the way of architecture. For at the heart of design, an architect has to sit by oneself—whether it's in the dining room or at the drafting table—generating data and absorbing it, thus setting the stage for another "Aha!" moment.

PHOTOGRAPHIC CREDITS

Figure numbers are noted on each picture caption.

Ron Pollard Photographs:

Tilley, Figs. 19–23; Beadles, Figs. 25–30, 32; Wood-Peterson, Figs. 33–37; and First Vradenburg, Figs. 40–44, Fig. 53.

Other Photographers:

Guy Burgess: Figs. 15, 46, 47
Don Etter: Figs. 3, 10, 11
Pedro Guerrero: Figs. 4-8
Kingsley Hammett, from Part II of a profile of Elizabeth Wright Ingraham in *Designer/Builder: A Journal of the Human Environment,* February 1998:
     Fig. 54
Ed LeCasse, courtesy of Ingraham and Ingraham Archives: Fig. 51
Thorney Lieberman, courtesy of Ingraham and Ingraham Archives: Fig. 52
Julius Shulman: Figs. 1, 2, 9

Archives and Collections:

Laura Gilpin, Colorado Springs Fine Arts Center 1938, photograph, 2002-8b; (Copyright) 1979, Amon Carter Museum, Fort Worth, Texas, Bequest of the artist. Collection of Taylor Museum, Colorado Springs Fine Arts Center: Fig. 13

Colorado Room Photo Files, Colorado Springs–Businesses, Special Collections, Tutt Library, Colorado College, Colorado Springs, Colorado: Fig. 14

Denver Public Library, Western History Collection, MSS Collection: Fig. 12

Ingraham and Ingraham Archives, courtesy of Elizabeth Wright Ingraham: Figs. 16, 17, 18, 50, 51, 52, 54

Appendix

Contractors, suppliers, and workmen for the Tilley, Beadles, Wood-Peterson, and First Vradenburg houses, as noted in Ingraham and Ingraham Archives. Companies are based in Colorado Springs, Colorado, unless otherwise noted.

Tilley House

In communications with the Tilleys and with contractors, the Ingrahams presented their role as principals in a variety of forms. The specifications listed Architect: Gordon Ingraham and Collaborator: Elizabeth Wright Ingraham. Printed stationery to several suppliers listed only Gordon Ingraham as architect. On December 9, 1948, the Ingrahams submitted a bill to Martha and Lew Tilley, which they signed: Louis Gordon Ingraham and Elizabeth Wright Ingraham, Designers.

Construction Systems:

Foundation and floor-based heating: James Bickley. The contract called for a combination radiant and convection system.
Plumbing:Olson-Benbow Plumbing and Heating Company.
Roofing: Heyse Sheet Metal and Roofing Company.
Electric: Whitney Electric Company.

Major Suppliers:

Glazing: Pikes Peak Glass Company.
Structural Clay Tile: The Summit Pressed Brick and Tile Company, Pueblo, Colorado, and the National Clay Products Company.
Lumber: H & S Lumber Company, Crissey Fowler Lumber Company, Newton Lumber Company, and Weller Lumber Company. Emil Hale provided railroad ties, the Homer and Rose Loban Sawmill provided rough lumber, and the Colorado Used Lumber Company provided used lumber.

The Tilleys were billed for services from H & G Welding; from Harry Groves for grading; from Western Iron, Metal and Machinery Company for supplies and services; and from Transit Mix for concrete.

Laborers:

John Wright [Elizabeth Wright Ingraham's brother]; Harry B. Osmun, mason; Gordon Ingraham.

Beadles House

The Ingrahams continued to use stationery for Gordon Ingraham, Architect. A statement of expenses to Robert Beadles for July, 1951, was marked: "Submitted from office of Gordon Ingraham by Elizabeth Wright Ingraham." An agreement dated March 15, 1951, states: "This agreement between Dr. and Mrs. Robert O. Beadles, hereinafter called the Owner, and, Gordon Ingraham, hereinafter called the Architect ..."

Construction Systems:

Foundation and floor-based heating: A. L. Ingwersen.
Concrete foundations and footings: S & C Enterprises.
Concrete floor: D. D. M. Concrete Company.
Plumbing: Olson Plumbing and Heating.
Roofing: Heyse Sheet Metal and Roofing Company.
Electric: Berwick Electric Company.

Major Suppliers:

Lumber: Denver Wood Products Company, Denver, Colorado; Abrahamson Lumber
Company; Weller Lumber Company; W. B. Bar Lumber Company, Denver, Colorado;
Newton Lumber Company; Colorado Used Lumber Company.
Millwork: Modern Millworking Company.
Glazing: Newton Lumber and Manufacturing Company.
Brick: S & C Enterprises, Inc., National Clay Products.
Paint: Paint Supply, Madsen Paint Service.
Tools: Frank Giver, Sears and Roebuck, General Hardware Company.
Other suppliers of services and goods: F. C. Borst, plastering; Harry Groves, excavating;
Lowell Meservey, hardware; Pikes Peak Fuel, gravel and rock;
H & G Welding, metalwork.

Laborers:

Bishop Nash, Gerald Smith, Dewey Dearing, Jim L. Potter, T. Von Stein, J. Robinson,
J. Plank, H. Ross, H. B. Osmun, H. W. Osmun, W. A. Floyd, Ed Bodenstein, Guy Matherly,
Don Blatten, Mac Okland.

Garrett Eckbo, a leading American modernist landscape designer, submitted a landscape
plan on behalf of his firm, Eckbo, Royston, and Williams, Los Angeles, California, on
March 12, 1952. Eckbo later (undated) sent the Ingrahams a handwritten note: "… it was
a pleasure to meet such nice people in Colorado Springs…," indicating he had visited the
Beadles site and had then received a letter from them declining his bid.

WOOD–PETERSON HOUSE

An agreement dated April 8, 1950, named Myron and June Wood as owners and Gordon
Ingraham as architect. Monthly statements to Myron Wood were submitted by "Gordon
Ingraham, Architect—Elizabeth Wright Ingraham."

Construction Systems:

Heating: James Bickley.
Plumbing: Olson-Benbow Plumbing and Heating Company.
Roofing: Heyse Sheet Metal and Roofing Company.
Electric: Whitney Electric Company.

Major Suppliers:

Glazing: Pikes Peak Glass Company.
Brick: National Clay Products.
Lumber: Newton Lumber Company, Crissey Fowler Lumber Company.
Concrete: D. M. Concrete Company, S & C Enterprises, Transit Mix Concrete Co.

Other suppliers of services and goods: Lowell Meservey, hardware; Donald Stickney, laying fire brick; Jend Industries, blue prints; Harry Grove, excavating and grading; R. L. Knight, excavating; W W. Funk, welding; H & G Welding.

Laborers:

G. Ingraham, B. Nash, B. Moery, Jon Lucie, Ed Johnson, B. Widmer, J. Norton, B. and A. Cribbs, Saad Sahawnah.

First Vradenburg House

The Ingrahams designed a house on the Mesa for William S. Roe and his family in 1951. Gordon Ingraham, architect, and William Roe, owner, formalized an agreement on June 12 of that year. The Ingrahams proceeded with construction drawings and bids to contractors. Work on the site commenced in early 1952 and continued into the fall. In the meantime, William Roe had suffered a sudden, debilitating illness. The Roe family could not complete and occupy the house. In 1953 George and Bee Vradenburg purchased the lot and the partially completed house. The Vradenburgs chose to expand and enhance the existing shell; the Ingrahams redesigned the house accordingly.

Construction Systems:

Foundations and walls: S & C Enterprises.
Heating: A. L. Ingwersen.
Plumbing: Olson Plumbing and Heating Company.
Roofing: Heyse Sheet Metal and Roofing Company.
Electric: Berwick Electric Company.

Major Suppliers:

Lumber: Crissey Fowler Lumber Company, Abrahamson Building and Supply Co.
Concrete: S & C Enterprises.
Brick contractor: Ralph Dallison.

Endnotes

1 Catherine Ingraham telephone interview with Elaine Freed, July 23, 2001.

2 Merritt Ierley, *The Comforts of Home: The American House and the Evolution of Modern Convenience*. New York: Clarkson Potter Publishers, 1999, p. 11.

3 Ibid., p. 193.

4 Deyan Sudjic, *Home: The Twentieth-Century House*. New York: Watson-Guptill Publications, 1999, pp. 8-9. Sudjic's early chapters trace the history of the modern house, offering an excellent summary and progression. Photographs and plan drawings amplify the text.

5 Magdalena Droste; Bauhaus-Arhiv. *Bauhaus:1919-1933*. Cologne, Germany: Taschen, 1998. This well-illustrated book traces the famous German school's interdisciplinary study, a program that had enormous influence in Europe and the United States.

6 James Steele, *R. M. Schindler*. Cologne, Germany: Taschen, 1999, pp. 170-73.

7 Sudjic, *Home: The Twentieth-Century House*, pp. 20-21. Sudjic points out that Mackintosh's Hill House, like many homes of the wealthy, was designed to accommodate the family in one set of rooms and the servants in another set—with some discreet overlap. There are, in fact, two households, one of which is very much behind the scenes.

8 *Encyclopedia of Modern Architecture*. New York: Harry Abrams, Inc., 1964, p. 35.

9 Esther McCoy, *Five California Architects*. New York: Reinhold Book Corporation, 1960. Reprinted Los Angeles: Hennessey & Ingalls, 1987.

10 Witold Rybczynski, *Home: A Short History of an Idea*. New York: Viking Penguin, 1986, pp. 51-75. Rybczynski describes at some length the strong influence of the seventeenth-century Dutch on modern ideas of home and family.

11 Terence Riley, *The (Un)Private House*. New York: Museum of Modern Art, 1999. Riley examines the evolution of home and family life in the last 400 years, with an emphasis on the radical changes in the last half of the twentieth century. Sudjic, in *Home: The Twentieth-Century House*, pp. 14-15, points to the centrality of technological invention in the evolution of modern house design.

12 Neil Levine, *The Architecture of Frank Lloyd Wright*. Princeton: Princeton University Press, 1996. See chapters I and II, pp. 1-57, for an analysis of Wright's Prairie houses. See also Dixie Legler and Christian Korab, photographer, *Prairie Style Houses and Gardens by Frank Lloyd Wright and the Prairie School*. New York: Stewart, Tabori & Chang, 1999, a recent illustrated survey of Prairie Style houses. Also Donald Hoffman, *Understanding Frank Lloyd Wright's Architecture*. New York: Dover Publications, Inc., 1995, for an analysis of Wright's work, with an emphasis on the Prairie Style era.

13 John Sergeant, *Frank Lloyd Wright's Usonian Houses: The Case for Organic Architecture*. New York: Watson-Guptill, 1976.

14 Frank Lloyd Wright, *The Natural House*. New York: Horizon Press, 1954, pp. 82-83.

15 Ibid., pp. 41-42.

16 Ibid., p. 79.

17 Ibid., pp. 51-52.

18 Ibid., p. 53.

19 Ibid., p. 108.

20 Ibid., p. 166.

21 Meryle Secrest, *Frank Lloyd Wright: A Biography*. New York: Alfred A. Knopf, 1992. Secrest writes of the Taliesin Fellowship, begun in 1932, as a school in which young students would learn all aspects of design in a hands-on and live-in situation.

22 Wright, *The Natural House*, pp. 197-98.

23 Sergeant, *Frank Lloyd Wright's Usonian Houses: The Case for Organic Architecture*, p. 140.

24 Ibid., p. 19.

25 Ibid., pp. 19-21.

26 Ibid., p. 27.

27 Ibid., p. 28.

28 Ibid., p. 30.

29 Gordon Ingraham, unpublished memoirs, 1992. Held by the Ingraham family.

30 Elizabeth Ingraham, personal communication, February 25, 2002.

31 Wright, *The Natural House*, p. 97.

32 Pierluigi Serraino and Julius Shulman, *Modernism Rediscovered*. Cologne, Germany: Taschen, 2000. The authors write that at mid-century the leading architectural journals were *Architectural Forum, Progressive Architecture, Architectural Record, House & Home, Interiors*, and *The AIA Journal. Architectural and Engineering News* and *Arts and Architecture* were among that group, as were regional magazines such as *Building Progress, Architecture West, Pacific Architect* and *Builder, Designers West*, and *Concrete Masonry Age*. Design magazines for the general public included *American Home, Architectural Digest, Better Homes and Gardens, Good Housekeeping, Ladies Home Journal, House and Garden*, and *House Beautiful. Life, Newsweek, Horizon, Look*, and *Sunset* also featured houses and design.

33 Elizabeth Ingraham, personal communication, February 25, 2002.

34 Ibid.

35 Ibid.

36 Ibid.

37 Elizabeth Ingraham interview with Elaine Freed, July 11, 2001.

38 Diane Wray, *Arapahoe Acres: An Architectural History, 1949-1957*. Englewood, CO: Wraycroft, Inc., 1997.

39 Ibid., p. 13.

40 Ibid., p. 13.

41 Jerry Ditto and Lanning Stern; Marvin Wax, photographer, *Design for Living: Eichler Homes*. San Francisco: Chronicle Books, 1995.

42 Esther McCoy, *Case Study Houses 1945-1962*, 2nd ed. Santa Monica, CA: Hennessey & Ingalls, Inc., 1977, p. 54.

43 Elizabeth Mock, *If You Want to Build a House*. New York: The Museum of Modern Art, 1946, p. 17.

44 Ibid., p. 11.

45 Ibid., p. 53.

46 Diane Maddex, *Frank Lloyd Wright's House Beautiful*. New York: Hearst Books, 2000. Elizabeth Gordon, editor of *House Beautiful*, celebrated Wright in several issues of the magazine in the beginning of the 1940s and into the 1960s. After meeting Wright at Taliesin West in 1946, she wrote and ran a twelve-page feature in the December issue (Maddex, p. 33). In April 1953 Gordon wrote an editorial, "The Threat to the Next America," the threat being the International Style (Maddex, p. 34). A November 1955 special issue featured Wright's work. After Wright died in April 1959, Gordon ran a memorial issue in October in his honor (Maddex, p. 38).

47 McCoy, *Case Study Houses*, 1945-1962, p. 1.

48 Ibid., p. 2.

49 Jean Graf and Don Graf, *Practical Houses for Contemporary Living*. New York: F. W. Dodge Corporation, 1953, p. 12.

50 Ibid., p. vi.

51 Wright, *The Natural House*, p. 51.

52 *Colorado Springs Free Press*, November 17, 1949.

53 McCoy, *Case Study Houses 1945–1962*, p. 5.

54 For information on the Ingrahams's journey west and their subsequent life in Colorado Springs, I have relied on Gordon's unpublished memoirs and on interviews with Elizabeth during 2001 and 2002, as well as other communications with her such as e-mail.

55 Elizabeth Ingraham interview with Elaine Freed, July 11, 2001.

56 Gordon Ingraham, unpublished memoirs, p. 92.

57 Ibid., p. 57.

58 Elizabeth Ingraham interview with Elaine Freed, July 11, 2001.

59 Gordon Ingraham, unpublished memoirs, p. 92.

[60] Ibid., pp. 93-98. In a July 19, 2001 interview with Elaine Freed, Elizabeth mentioned many of the same artist friends.

[61] Max Lanner, *Historical Notes on the Music Department of Colorado College (1874-1959)*. Edited and with *Additional Notes for the Period 1959–1994* by Richard J. Agee. Colorado Springs, CO: Colorado College, 1994. See pp. 21-37 for a discussion of the 1930s through 1950s.

[62] Marshall Sprague, *Newport in the Rockies: The Life and Good Times of Colorado Springs*. Denver: Sage Books, 1961. Sprague's lively profile of Colorado Springs remains the definitive summary of the city's first century. For an account of the arts scene, see Chapter Twenty, pp. 282-307.

[63] Hunter Frost, *Boardman Robinson*. Topsham, ME, and Colorado Springs, CO: Tiverton Press, 1996. This is a commemorative publication to celebrate Robinson's life with a retrospective that included events and exhibitions at the Colorado Springs Fine Arts Center and Fountain Valley School.

[64] Johanne Coiner interview with Elaine Freed, December 28, 2001. In this series of ten paintings, Robinson used auto paints to achieve a lively color that would not fade. The paintings are now in the collection of the Colorado Springs Fine Arts Center and exhibited in Gates Common Room, Palmer Hall, at Colorado College.

[65] Ibid. To say Robinson resigned is to put a good face on the situation. Mitchell A. Wilder, the art center's director, was intent on moving toward abstraction and a more modern image. "He fired Gramps," Coiner said. She is sympathetic to a point with Wilder's efforts to redirect the center but insistent that Robinson's era — the 1930s and 1940s — was the region's Golden Age for the arts. Coiner sees two forces at work in the city at that time: exceptional artistic talent and great wealth. Money from Cripple Creek gold mining was still concentrated in a few hands and attracted other wealthy people.

[66] Martha Tilley interview with Elaine Freed, June 5, 2001.

[67] David G. Turner and Robert Mark Harris, *Modern Deco: An Architectural Guidebook for the Colorado Springs Fine Arts Center*. Colorado Springs, CO: Fine Arts Center, 1996, p. 12. Mitchell Wilder was the first director of the Taylor Museum collection, which is a part of the center, and then assumed directorship of the entire center from 1946 to 1953.

[68] *Gazette Telegraph*, January 12, 1952.

[69] John Hazlehurst interview with Elaine Freed, December 21, 2001. A collector and journalist, Hazlehurst believes Robinson to be the most brilliant American draftsman of the twentieth century. Among the Colorado Springs artists of the 1950s era, he finds modernist Emerson Woelffer the most talented. He considered Lawrence Barrett a "fantastic teacher and technician." Hazlehurst also admired Mitchell Wilder, who was facing big problems at the Fine Arts Center. "It was stagnant and needed to change. The founding giants had died off."

[70] *Gazette Telegraph*, January 22, 1952.

[71] *Colorado Springs Free Press*, January 17, 1952, p. 2.

[72] *Colorado Springs Free Press*, February 3, 1952. When the dust had settled, the *Free Press* did a long, adulatory piece on the newly reconstituted Fine Arts Center, describing new programs and underscoring the need for change.

[73] *Colorado Springs Free Press*, January 5, 1950.

[74] *Colorado Springs Free Press*, December 16, 1949. The city's leaders mobilized: J. Douglas Crouch was chair of military affairs for the Chamber of Commerce. Russell D. Law headed a special committee for securing the United States Air Force Academy. William Thayer Tutt, H. Chase Stone, and General O. H. Griswold were part of the team.

[75] *Colorado Springs Free Press*, December 4, 1949. On page 1: "Camp Carson will be rebuilt in a multi-million-dollar program converting it into a permanent military installation named Fort Kit Carson." On page 4: "... the deal shows some smart thinking by local men who are going all out to insure Colorado Springs an adequate future water supply."

[76] *Gazette Telegraph*, September 23, 1949, p. 1.

[77] Both the *Gazette Telegraph* and *Colorado Springs Free Press* documented these national and international developments during 1949 and 1950. As external events threatened, the local scene grew increasingly rosy, and in fact the two were connected: the city's federal installations all aimed at fending off global communism.

78 *Colorado Springs Free Press*, January 6, 1950, p. 1. Clay Banta was honored as "Outstanding Young Man of the Year." He was president of the Junior Chamber of Commerce.

79 Report: *Military Down-Sizing: The Potential Effects on the Military and Civilian Populations in the Colorado Springs Area, Colorado*, prepared by Science Applications International Corporation, Santa Barbara, CA, November, 1994. Figure 1, Economic Sectors - Employment (El Paso County) 1970, shows a pie graph of government payroll percentage: Federal Civilian (8.1%); State and Local (8.7%), Military (31.6%).

80 John Hazlehurst interview with Elaine Freed, December 21, 2001.

81 Sudjic, *Home: The Twentieth-Century House*, p. 76.

82 Ingraham and Ingraham Archives.

83 Elizabeth Ingraham interview with Elaine Freed, July 19, 2001.

84 Ibid.

85 Ibid.

86 Gordon Ingraham, unpublished memoirs, p. 95. Recalling his attitudes in 1948, Gordon said: "I know that I took on the role of the architect strongly. I know that I became immersed in the flavor of Wright and followed his precepts avidly. I know that I tried to keep a vision of his principles in my mind."

87 Catherine Ingraham telephone interview with Elaine Freed, July 23, 2001.

88 Ibid.

89 Ibid.

90 Ibid.

91 Ibid.

92 Ibid.

93 Anna Ingraham interview with Elaine Freed, July 7, 2001.

94 Christine Ingraham interview with Elaine Freed, July 8, 2001.

95 Ibid.

96 Catherine Ingraham interview.

97 Ibid.

98 Christine Ingraham interview.

99 Ibid.

100 Ibid.

101 Michael Ingraham interview with Elaine Freed, June 27, 2001.

102 Ibid.

103 Ibid.

104 Christine Ingraham interview.

105 Anna Ingraham interview.

106 Catherine Ingraham interview.

107 Ibid.

108 Michael Ingraham interview.

109 Ibid.

110 Martha Tilley interview with Elaine Freed, June 5, 2001.

111 Ibid.

112 Ibid.

113 Ibid.

114 Ibid.

115 Ibid.

116 Robert and Mildred Beadles interview with Elaine Freed, January 17, 2001.

117 Material about the house came from Robert and Mildred Beadles in interview. I visited the house several times.

118 Eric Bransby telephone interview with Elaine Freed, January 26, 2002.

119 Mildred Beadles interview with Elaine Freed, January 17, 2001.

[120] Robert and Mildred Beadles interview.

[121] Ibid.

[122] Ibid.

[123] Ibid.

[124] Robert and Mildred Beadles interview.

[125] My descriptions of the Wood-Peterson house are based on interviews with E. R. Peterson and Judith Peterson as well as visits to the house.

[126] E. R. Peterson interview with Elaine Freed, August 28, 2001.

[127] Ibid.

[128] Judith Peterson interview with Elaine Freed, August 24, 2001.

[129] To gather material for the first Vradenburg house, I interviewed current owners Kent Borges and Stephanie DiCenzo and visited the house several times.

[130] Kent Borges and Stephanie DiCenzo interview with Elaine Freed, November 28, 2001.

[131] Ibid.

[132] Anna Ingraham interview.

[133] Michael Ingraham interview

[134] Christine Ingraham interview.

[135] Gordon Ingraham, unpublished memoirs, p. 128.

[136] Catherine Ingraham interview.

[137] Christine Ingraham interview.

[138] Michael Ingraham interview.

[139] Anna Ingraham interview.

[140] Gordon Ingraham, unpublished memoirs, p. 137.

[141] Elizabeth Ingraham interview with Elaine Freed, March 13, 2002.

[142] Ibid.

[143] Ibid.

[144] Ibid.

[145] Ibid.

[146] Ibid.

[147] Ibid.

[148] Ibid.

[149] Dawn and Bradley Wilde interview with Elaine Freed, June 12, 2002.

[150] Cynthia Davidson, "Elizabeth Wright Ingraham Reaches Out to the Landscape with Rugged Forms," *Architectural Record*, February 2001, pp. 116-19.

[151] Michael Ingraham interview.

[152] Christine Ingraham interview.

[153] Anna Ingraham interview.

[154] Catherine Ingraham interview.

[155] Michael Ingraham interview.

Bibliography

Books

Brown, Jane. *The Modern Garden*. New York: Princeton Architectural Press, 2000.

Chanzit, Gwen Finkel. *Herbert Bayer and Modernist Design in America*. Ann Arbor/London: UMI Research Press, 1987.

Creighton, Thomas H., and Katherine Morrow Ford. *Contemporary Houses: Evaluated by Their Owners*. New York: Reinhold Publishing Corporation, 1961.

Ditto, Jerry, Lanning Stern, and Marvin Wax, photographer. *Design for Living: Eichler Homes*. San Francisco: Chronicle Books, 1995.

Droste, Magdalena; Bauhaus Archiv. *Bauhaus 1919–1933*. Cologne, Germany: Taschen, 1999.

Etter, Don D. *Denver Going Modern: A Photographic Essay on the Imprint of the International Style on Denver Residential Architecture*. Limited edition of 1,000; copy number 487. Denver: Graphic Impressions, Inc., 1977.

Frampton, Kenneth. *American Masterworks: The Twentieth Century House*. Edited by Kenneth Frampton and David Larkin. New York: Rizzoli International Publications, Inc., 1995.

Friedman, Alice T. *Women and the Making of the Modern House: A Social and Architectural History*. New York: Harry N. Abrams, Inc., 1998.

Frost, Hunter. *Boardman Robinson*. Topsham, ME, and Colorado Springs, CO: Tiverton Press, 1996.

Girouard, Mark. *Life in the English Country House: A Social and Architectural History*. New Haven and London: Yale University Press, 1978.

Graf, Jean, and Don Graf, A.I.A. *Practical Houses for Contemporary Living*. New York: F. W. Dodge Corporation, 1953.

Guggenheimer, Tobias S. *A Taliesin Legacy*. New York: Van Nostrand Reinhold, 1995.

Hoffman, Donald. *Understanding Frank Lloyd Wright's Architecture*. New York: Dover Publications, Inc., 1995.

Ierley, Merritt. *The Comforts of Home: The American House and the Evolution of Modern Convenience*. New York: Clarkson N. Potter, Crown Publishing Group, 1999.

Jackson, Lesley. *The New Look: Design in the Fifties*. New York: Thames and Hudson, Inc., 1991.

Lanner, Max. *Historical Notes on the Music Department of Colorado College (1874–1959)*. Edited and with *Additional Notes for the Period 1959–1994* by Richard J. Agee. Colorado Springs, CO: Colorado College, 1994.

Legler, Dixie, and Christian Korab, photographer. *Prairie Style: Houses and Gardens by Frank Lloyd Wright and the Prairie School*. New York: Stewart, Tabori & Chang, 1999.

Levine, Neil. *The Architecture of Frank Lloyd Wright*. Princeton: Princeton University Press, 1996.

Maddex, Diane. *Frank Lloyd Wright's House Beautiful*. New York: Hearst Books, 2000.

McCoy, Esther. *Case Study Houses 1945–1962*. Second edition. Santa Monica, CA: Hennessey & Ingalls, Inc., 1977.

___. *Five California Architects*. New York: Reinhold Book Corporation, 1960. Reprint, Los Angeles: Hennessey & Ingalls, Inc., 1987.

Mock, Elizabeth B. *If You Want to Build a House*. New York: The Museum of Modern Art, 1946; distributed by Simon and Schuster, Inc., New York.

Musick, Archie. *Musick Medley: Intimate Memories of a Rocky Mountain Art Colony*. Colorado Springs, CO: Jane and Archie Musick, 1971.

Peter, John. *Masters of Modern Architecture*. New York: Bonanza Books, a division of Crown Publishers, Inc., by arrangement with George Braziller, Inc., 1958.

Pevsner, Nikolaus. *The Sources of Modern Architecture and Design*. New York and Toronto: Oxford University Press, 1968.

Riley, Terence. *The (Un)private House*. New York: The Museum of Modern Art, 1999; distributed by Harry N. Abrams, Inc., New York.

Rybczynski, Witold. *Home: A Short History of an Idea*. New York: Viking Penguin, Inc., 1986.

Schezen, Roberto. *Adolf Loos: Architecture 1903–1932*. New York: The Monacelli Press, Inc., 1996.

Schultze, Franz. *Mies van der Rohe: A Critical Biography*. Chicago: The University of Chicago Press, 1985.

Scully, Vincent, Jr. *Modern Architecture: The Architecture of Democracy*. Revised. New York: George Braziller, Inc., 1961.

Secrest, Meryle. *Frank Lloyd Wright: A Biography*. New York: Alfred A. Knopf, 1992.

Sergeant, John. *Frank Lloyd Wright's Usonian Houses: The Case for Organic Architecture*. New York. Whitney Library of Design, 1976. Reprint, Watson Guptill Publications, New York, 1984.

Serraino, Pierluigi, and Julius Shulman. *Modernism Rediscovered*. Cologne, Germany: Taschen, 2000.

Smith, Kathryn. *Frank Lloyd Wright's Taliesin and Taliesin West*. New York: Harry N. Abrams, Inc., 1997.

____. *Schindler House*. New York: Harry N. Abrams, Inc., 2001.

Sprague, Marshall. *Newport in the Rockies: The Life and Good Times of Colorado Springs*. Denver: Sage Books, 1961.

Steele, James. *R. M. Schindler*. Edited and designed by Peter Gossel. Cologne, Germany: Taschen, 1999.

Sudjic, Deyan, with Tulga Beyerle. *Home: The Twentieth-Century House*. New York: Watson-Guptill Publications, a division of BPI Communications, Inc., 1999.

Turner, David G., and Robert Mark Harris. *Modern Deco: An Architectural Guidebook for the Colorado Springs Fine Arts Center*. Colorado Springs, CO: Colorado Springs Fine Arts Center, 1996.

Walker, Lester. *American Shelter: An Illustrated Encyclopedia of the American Home*. Woodstock, NY: The Overlook Press, 1981.

Wiseman, Carter. *Twentieth-Century American Architecture: The Buildings and Their Makers*. New York/London: W. W. Norton & Company, Inc., 2000. Previous edition published under the title *Shaping a Nation: Twentieth-Century American Architecture and Its Makers*.

Wray, Diane. *Arapahoe Acres: An Architectural History 1949–1957*. Englewood, CO: Wraycroft, Inc., 1997.

Wright, Frank Lloyd. *An Autobiography*. New York: Horizon Press, 1977. Revised; originally published in 1932.

___. *The Natural House*. New York: Horizon Press, 1954.

Periodicals

Bone, Eugenia. "Building Holistically." *Metropolis*, January/February, 1997, pp. 76–79.

Davidson, Cynthia. "Elizabeth Wright Ingraham Reaches Out to the Landscape with Rugged Forms." *Architectural Record*. February, 2001, pp. 116–19.

International Architecture Yearbook, No. 3, 1997, pp. 19–20, 306–09, 425. The Images Publishing Group, Pty. Ltd., Australia.

"Profile: Elizabeth Wright Ingraham," *Designer/Builder: A Journal of the Human Environment*, Part I, Vol. IV, No. 9, January, 1998, pp. 4–11; Part II, Vol. IV, No. 10, February, 1998, pp. 4–9.

Photo Index

Chapter 1

Chapter 2

Chapter 3

Chapter 4

Afterword